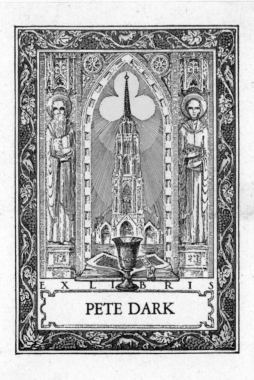

INSIDE ROME

WITH THE GERMANS

THE MACMILLAN COMPANY
NEW YORK · BOSTON · CHICAGO · DALLAS
ATLANTA · SAN FRANCISCO

MACMILLAN AND CO., Limited
LONDON · BOMBAY · CALCUTTA · MADRAS
MELBOURNE

THE MACMILLAN COMPANY
OF CANADA, Limited
TORONTO

INSIDE ROME
WITH
THE GERMANS

By JANE SCRIVENER

O Roma nobilis
Orbis et domina
Cunctarum urbium
Excellentissima.

—*Ancient pilgrim chant*

NEW YORK
THE MACMILLAN COMPANY
1945

A WARTIME BOOK

THIS COMPLETE EDITION IS PRODUCED
IN FULL COMPLIANCE WITH THE GOVERN-
MENT'S REGULATIONS FOR CONSERVING
PAPER AND OTHER ESSENTIAL MATERIALS.

PRINTED IN THE UNITED STATES OF AMERICA

To E. C. H.

I promised to write this diary for you.
Here it is, with love.

FOREWORD

By Carlton J. H. Hayes

Late American Ambassador to Spain

How fortunate that among the very few Americans who remained in Rome throughout the war there was an alert and talented lady who had a literary flair and kept a diary! She writes under the pseudonym of Jane Scrivener, but this, as I shall presently explain, is the only "pseudo" thing about it. It is an eyewitness account, as authentic as it is vivid.

As background, one may recall that Mussolini and his Fascists, in concert with Hitler, had plunged Italy into war against France and Great Britain in June, 1940, and against the United States in December, 1941. By the spring of 1943 Italy was overwhelmed by misfortunes at home and abroad. Axis rout in North Africa was being followed by Allied invasion of Sicily, while within Italy the masses of the population were suffering intensely and Mussolini had become a mere puppet of the Germans who already occupied and terrorized the country.

"Jane Scrivener" was an old friend of my wife and myself, and while we were in Spain we received letters from her giving us lively impressions of what was transpiring in Rome. She described with special vigor the Allied air attack of July 19, 1943—the efficacious bombing of railway yards and freight station, the wrecking of a populous workingman's quarter, the ripping up of a cemetery, the demolishing of the famous old basilica of St. Lawrence-Outside-the-Walls. She conveyed a sense of the thrill of horror that immediately ran through the city, of the increasing tension of the ensuing "hot July days," and of the historic character of the ten-hour session of the Fascist Council on July 24th and the King's announcement two days later that Mussolini had been dismissed and Marshal Badoglio was prime minister. Of the scene on this day, she wrote: "The joy of the Italians on being rid of Fascism gives Rome a carnival air. Torn fragments of Mussolini's portraits lie like snow on the pavements. People laugh and talk in the streets as they have not done for years. Perfect strangers greet and congratulate one another. '*Now* we can say what we like, with no fear of spies,' they joyously exclaim. Fascist emblems are hacked from public buildings to the accompaniment of cheers and applause. The city is covered with posters: 'Evviva il Re!' 'Evviva Badoglio!' 'Evviva la libertà!' Rome, in her long history, has never known quite such a day."

Forty-five days passed, and on September 8, 1943, Marshal Badoglio concluded the armistice with the Allies. But this did not mean the delivery of Rome. Quite the opposite. It was the Germans and not the Italians who were in effective military control of the city, and the Germans had no intention of surrendering it or treating it as an "open city." Nor were the Allies in any position then, or for a long time afterwards, to liberate Rome. For months their offensive bogged down many miles south. It was not until June 5, 1944, after a lapse of nine frightful months, that "Jane Scrivener" saw in Rome the first Allied soldiers—four American boys in a jeep—and knew that at long last the Eternal City was free and secure.

It is the day-to-day events of those nine months from the Armistice of September, 1943, to the Allied arrival in June, 1944, which the diary, now published, records. They were months of dreadful suspense, of alternating hope and despair, and of steadily increasing misery. Food and fuel grew ever scarcer, while refugees and escaped war prisoners overcrowded the cold, hungry city. Looting and assassination, and dire Nazi reprisals, added to the terror and havoc wrought by Allied bombs which missed their military targets. And occasionally, amid so much tragedy, the occupying Germans unwittingly provided a comic touch.

All this is depicted in "Jane Scrivener's" diary with immediacy and spontaneity, and with an excellent eye for both fact and form. Appropriately depicted, too, is the role of the Pope and the Vatican as Rome's bulwarks during the whole trying time. The Vatican found food for the starving. It eased physical and spiritual hardships. It guarded treasures of literature and art. Pope Pius XII stood forth against the Nazis as, centuries earlier, Pope Leo I had stood forth—and saved Rome—against Attila and the Huns.

For an understanding of the Pope's position vis-à-vis the Nazi forces in Rome, and of the diary's frequent references to it, one should bear in mind that the Lateran Treaty which the Italian Government had concluded with the Holy See on February 11, 1929, and which therefore was binding in international law, accorded to the Pope certain temporal rights and jurisdiction in Rome. Consequently, when the Germans took full and undisguised military possession of the city in 1943, they were obliged not only to repress local agents and supporters of the Italian Government of Marshal Badoglio, which they could do with their armies and police, but also to deal with a Pope against whom they hesitated to employ force and yet whom they discovered to be adamant about his rights.

By the terms of the Lateran Treaty, that part of Rome which comprised the Vatican and St. Peter's—the so-called Vatican City —was an independent sovereign state of the Pope's; and in it, throughout the war, resided diplomatic representatives of almost all the United Nations as well as of the Axis. But this was not all. In addition, the Treaty provided for papal governance, through the international usage of "extraterritoriality," of a considerable number of properties in Rome and its environs outside of Vatican City. These included the basilicas of St. John Lateran, St. Paul's-Outside-the-Walls, and St. Mary Major, together with all buildings connected with them; the palace of St. Calixtus in Trastevere; the papal summer residence and farms at Castel Gandolfo; the Augustinian college of Santa Monica and other buildings on the Janiculum; the old Church of St. Michael and its neighboring convent; the Jesuit headquarters and house of retreats; the College of the Propaganda; the church and convent of St. Onofrio; the Bambin Gesù hospital; the Ukrainian and Rumanian colleges; the palaces of the Chancery and the Datary in the center of Rome; that of the Propagation of the Faith in the Piazza di Spagna; that of the Holy Office near St. Peter's; the Vicariat in the Via della Pigna; and "Raphael's House" in the Via della Conciliazione.

Besides these "extraterritorial" properties, certain others were stipulated in the Lateran Treaty as being free from expropriation because owned by the Holy See, although otherwise subject to the jurisdiction of the Italian State. These were the buildings attached to the basilica of the Twelve Apostles and to the churches of St. Andrew and St. Charles; the Gregorian University; the Biblical, Archaeological, and Oriental Institutes; the Russian Seminary; the Lombard College; the two palaces of St. Apollinarius; and the House of Retreats of Saints John and Paul.

The papal properties, thus scattered all over Rome, made it no easier for the Nazis there. Indeed, had it not been for the Lateran Treaty and the Vatican's neutrality during the war, the German occupation might have been much worse than it was both for the anti-Fascist Italians and for the Allies. "Neutrality on the part of the Pope," the author of the diary has written, "did not signify any sympathy by him for Fascism or Nazism. These totalitarian doctrines already stood condemned, (a) by the moral law, which he constantly preached, and (b) by such specific papal encyclicals as *Non Abbiamo Bisogno* and *Mit Brennender Sorge*. It has always been the policy of the Holy See to observe neutrality towards whatever Power might have effective military control of the city of Rome, in order to maintain contact with its own representatives abroad and with the Catholic hierarchy in all parts of the world. It was only because of this neutrality that the Pope was able to carry on multitudinous good works for suffering mankind during the course of the war, works which ranged from supplying war prisoners everywhere, regardless of race or nationality, with material and spiritual help, to providing aid for devastated areas and feeding the starving in Rome. (When the Allies entered the city, the Holy See was furnishing daily meals for 15,000.) For the well-being of Christian peoples, the Holy See has always negotiated even with the worst pagan rulers."

A few final words about "Jane Scrivener" herself. Her pseudonym should not arouse any apprehension. I have known her and her family for a goodly number of years. She is an American citizen and a cultivated lady, who has engaged in numerous educational activities in Europe, especially in France and Italy. For many years she has lived in Rome, and I remember well, when I was last there—in the spring of 1938—how disgusted and ironical she was about the preparations then being made by Mussolini to welcome Hitler on a visit to the capital of Christendom.

She is a staunch American, as the diary amply demonstrates. She is also a Catholic religious, and it is this fact which explains her remaining in Rome during the war and her having the intimate knowledge which she has recorded. She knows her Rome thoroughly, and she has had many contacts through the religious house where she lived, and likewise through the Vatican where she worked on "prisoners' relief." Every night she would write what in the daytime her attentive eyes and ears had learned.

She began and continued the day-to-day writing in her diary without any thought of its ever being published. But the parts of it which she put in personal letters to my wife, and managed to get through to Spain, so fascinated us that we urged her to let the public have access to the whole story. She finally agreed, and despatched the manuscript by special courier from Rome to Madrid, whence I brought it to the United States. I am delighted that it now becomes available to the many who, I feel sure, will find it a most interesting and illuminating "inside" story of crucial war months in Rome.

We have seen and heard many things these days. Here is my diary—for what it is worth.

The whole city shuddered with fear of a repetition of the bombings of July and August when, at midday today, the siren wailed and the boom and thud of distant explosions were heard. However, word soon went round that it was Frascati, as the attack was clearly visible from the Janiculum. Of course for months the Castelli had been overflowing with German troops, and sooner or later were bound to be bombed. This, then, was it. Flying fortresses poured explosives on all the neighbouring townlets: Albano, Marino, Castel Gandolfo, Lanuvio, Genzano, Velletri, Ciampino and its airport, but most of all on Frascati. It went on for an hour and ten minutes, and at the end of that time Frascati lay in ruins. Dear, ancient, crowded, noisy, gay little Frascati was wiped out. One thousand of its inhabitants lay dead, as against 150 Germans. Was it worth it? Marshal Kesselring, the German commander in chief, crawled from under the ruins of his quarters unharmed. Yes, they got that house too. The Cathedral, the square in front of it, Cardinal of York's fountain and the shops surrounding it, the church of Gesù and that of St. Roch, several convents, the bank, the Bishop's palace and the Salesians' big school at Villa Sora suffered severely. The historic villas, Frascati's most aristocratic feature, were nearly all damaged. The famous Jesuit College at Villa Mondragone was out of the line of the attack, so members of the community there, together with the Salesians and the Camaldolese from Tusculum, came down into the town, dug survivors out of the wreckage and buried the dead. The buildings around Piazza Roma where the railway and tram terminus used to be were swept away, as well as the three hotels, the Roma, the Tusculum, and the Park. Desolation and a thick cloud of white dust settled on Frascati, as the departing planes were lost in the blue. It is gone, and

[1]

forever, I think; gone with its dark little shops, its grocers and bakers, its umbrella mender who also sold mousetraps, its one electrician and its solitary watchmaker (who always said *"a Roma"* when you wanted anything), its hard-working winter population, its patient postmistress, its swarms of school children and its crowds of riotous *villeggianti* in summer. It is all silent and dead. There it lies. The wreckage of war.

At half past seven the news of the armistice broke. The Roman radio broadcast Eisenhower's statement and Badoglio's short dignified address to the Italian people. Armistice! A sigh of relief went up from the crowds around the loud-speakers. Then a pause. People looked at each other questioningly—Armistice or Armageddon? What about the Germans? In country places, such as Cori, up in the hills, where there were no Germans, the rejoicings knew no bounds; bonfires were lit, and the peasants and village folk rioted to their heart's content. But Rome was quiet. Martial law was still in force, and by 9.30 the streets were deserted. But there were plenty of celebrations indoors. In more than one place the health of the Allies was drunk. The Germans in the city lay low that night, distinctly apprehensive; there were not many of them, and they awaited orders.

Thursday September 9th

One awoke with a stab of anxiety. True, the burden of thirty-eight long months of war had been lifted, but what would the day bring forth?

News came in hectic gusts hour by hour. In the papers there was a chorus of approval of Badoglio's measures. The German radio let loose a flood of invective against the "vile treason of the Italians." People overflowing with optimism began to talk English freely on the telephone. Yes, it was all over. The Italians would have to hold out for just one week and then the Allies would be here; they had dropped leaflets to that effect. Everything was lovely. Suddenly we heard the booming of big guns. "The British fleet off Ostia," said friends who had come in to discuss the situation. "No, it's the Germans blowing up their ammunition dumps because they can't take it away with them." But are they? It is strange to be in the heart of these things and to know really nothing about them. The radio makes no allusion to them.

In the afternoon it clouded over, and the morning's optimism clouded over too. By 3 P.M. shops were shutting uncannily. Afraid of looting? But by whom? The Italians aren't going to start that, surely? And the Germans? But they say the garrison of Rome is strong, and then there's Cadorna with his whole division out at Bracciano. Surely the Germans are well in hand? . . .

By six, knots of people collected in the streets and word went round in horrified whispers that the Germans were marching into Rome. "They are at Ponte Milvio." "They're in Piazza San Giovanni." A lot of Italian soldiers hastily put on civilian clothes. The Roman barracks were evacuated. Rumour said that Badoglio had escaped from Rome and had sent his daughter to Switzerland. Civilians went home and shut the great doors of their houses—those *portoni*, the characteristic feature of Italian buildings, which serve them in the office of a wall or as a moat defensive to a house, and close their porte-cochères hermetically.

10 P.M. The siren: sinister, depressing. Then bombs. So that was the German answer to the armistice. Thud. Thud. Thud. On Rome. Near the University; near the Vatican City in Via Sisto Quinto; near Via Cassia and near the Madonna del Riposo. In half an hour it was over, and the silence of the streets was broken only by rifle and revolver shots. Rome slept as best it could.

Friday September 10th

The 8 o'clock broadcast announced that Badoglio had placed General Caviglia in command of the city. He is a man past seventy, upright, incorruptible, capable and universally admired and respected; as a non-Fascist he used to be suggested as the only possible substitute for Mussolini in the days when anti-Fascism was living underground. One felt confident that, with him, all would be well.

Guns sound in the far distance. Some German soldiers pass down Via dei Mille, handcuffed and under guard. So much the better. It seems that the *Granatieri* met oncoming Germans out near La Cecchignola on the Via Ardeatina. We knew that in the

[3]

open country beyond La Cecchignola, there had been a large German camp for over a year.

By 11 o'clock it was made known that Caviglia had negotiated with the Germans for their withdrawal to a point farther north, and that they would, in consequence, not enter Rome. Excellent. We should now be free of them without further fighting. Everybody was hopeful. One knew that Caviglia would manage them. How wise of Badoglio to have appointed him. The firing died down in the distance.

By midday St. Peter's was shut. When, in the memory of man, had it been shut in the daytime? Still, of course it was wise. If a panic-stricken crowd had rushed into it for protection, the situation might well have become complicated. It looked very desolate. The same with the Vatican City: Porta Santa Anna was hermetically closed. At the Arco delle Campane gate a Swiss with businesslike rifle and bayonet, instead of his medieval pike, guarded the entrance; in like manner there was one at the closed Portone di Bronzo. Palatine Guards reinforced the Swiss, who are not very numerous. The commander of the Noble Guard placed six of his men on duty night and day, in turns, near the Pope's person, and a number of them moved into residence in the Vatican so as to be close at hand, as anything might happen in the little Pontifical State.

At 1 o'clock, the siren again. The siren? Yes, the siren. But we thought— — Bombs seemed to fall close beside us. Then the whistle and thud of shells echoed over the city. It was unmistakable: they were using artillery and shelling the heights of Rome. Roman artillery answered from the Aventine, the Palatine, the Caelian, the Janiculum, the Pincian. A German shell screeched across Ponte Cavour and crashed into the Palazzo di Giustizia. Via Frattina, the Trinità, S. Maria della Pace were also hit. On the line of the Tiber, at San Gregorio, on the hills, Italian gunners were hard at work.

By degrees the fighting moved in from the country, down Via Ardeatina and Via Laurentina, past Tre Fontane, and neared St. Paul's. Machine guns, rifles and hand grenades came into play. When the fight was hottest, wounded men were carried into Santa Sabina, the great Dominican convent on the Aventine.

Italian soldiers appeared in disorder, straggling in along the

Lungotevere, dusty, hungry and bedraggled. But there were no officers. The men reported that their officers said: "We have no more ammunition. Do what you can for yourselves, boys," and left them. As might have been expected, the Germans had used their negotiations with Caviglia as a blind, and instead of withdrawing, advanced firing on the Italians. They had also obtained possession of the cipher used in giving army orders to Italian officers, and a large number of the latter received instructions not to fight if they met the Germans; others were directed to present themselves at headquarters in mufti. The men were ready to fight the oncoming Germans, but they were not led. This elimination of officers was characteristic of German methods; it was achieved principally by their Fifth Column in Rome.

The Roman artillerymen, however, knowing nothing of what had happened at Cecchignola, replied fiercely for nearly two hours when the Germans shelled the city. Armoured cars rushed through the streets to meet the enemy, only to be turned back at the gates.

But it was merely outside Porto San Paolo that the treacherous orders were obeyed. Inside the city fighting went on practically everywhere. The Hotel Continental, near the station, was attacked by Italian troops and civilians armed with machine guns, and defended by Fascists and Germans firing from the windows. Observers crowded roofs and terraces. On the narrow gallery at the top of the tall bell tower of San Camillo, a slender figure was visible outlined against the sky. In his dark cassock, with the vivid red cross on his breast, that *Camillino* priest stood watching, watching, and praying; he seemed the embodiment of a guardian spirit mourning over the strife below.

A ferocious encounter took place near the Ministry of the Interior in Via Agostino Depretis, with Fascists and Germans inside, Italians attacking from the street. Near the Circus Maximus a platoon of Germans took advantage of the newly constructed tunnel for the underground railway, dived into it and emerged at the Colosseum, only to find resolute Italians at the other end, awaiting them with hand genades and revolvers.

It all recalled those lines in *Le Cid* when the hero is describing their battle against the Moors, in the dark:

Et chacun seul témoin des grands coups qu'il donnait
Ne pouvait discerner où le sort inclinait.

Certainly the isolated groups engaged in the disorderly struggle knew nothing of what was happening to the others. Blood ran in the streets near the railway station, particularly in Via Massimo d'Azeglio and Via Cavour, as well as in Via Nazionale, Via del Tritone, Piazza Venezia and Corso Umberto Primo. Wherever Germans were seen they were set upon. Clashes were violent in the old Trastevere, home of violence in all ages. When it had subsided somewhat an old *Trasteverino* stooped over a dead body, looked about helplessly, then went across the street and commandeered a fruit seller's handcart, laboriously placed the corpse on it and wheeled it off to the nearest hospital. Many handcarts in Rome today were used in a like manner.

Armoured cars seemed to be everywhere at the same time, some manned by Italians, some by Germans, and all of them firing. The whole thing was a mixture of riot, civil war, real war and anarchy. Shops were shut and doors were closed, but that did not prevent looting, particularly along the line of march between Porta San Paolo and the Circus Maximus. The Central Market was stripped bare. Over in the Testaccio quarter storehouses were broken open, and not only did the Germans themselves loot, but they encouraged the bewildered populace to follow their example. Some of them took photographs of the poor creatures carrying away cheeses and parcels of *pasta*. Worse still, they broke open the wine cellars beneath the Testaccio hill, drank all they wanted, and then invited the public to do the same. The submerged tenth flocked to the spot with cans, bottles, saucepans, anything that would hold liquid, and took full advantage of the opportunity. Two Dominican Fathers who happened to be passing tried to summon the police by telephone but, as might have been expected, no police were forthcoming. They had taken cover indoors. The two priests did what they could, unaided, to stem the tide of theft and drunkenness; and, strange to say, their words were listened to and they went home unharmed.

The Germans, at last, in rather straggling formation, marched down Via dei Trionfi, past the Arch of Constantine and down

Via del Impero to Piazza di Venezia, where machine guns had been barking all afternoon. Another detachment of them came in by Porta San Giovanni, and down Via Merulana. They passed beneath the walls of St. John Lateran, making toward St. Mary Major's (Santa Maria Maggiore), and I think those ancient walls remembered old unhappy far-off things, very like those of today: Guiscard's Normans wrecking that neighbourhood in 1084, and Bourbon's Lutheran hordes in 1527, were after all, not so very unlike Hitler's Huns riding in on their tanks and lorries, driving the defeated Romans before them as they went.

Unconscious of what had really taken place, university students dashed through the streets shouting: "Come on to Piazza Colonna, to cheer for our men!" When they got there they found themselves looking into the muzzles of machine guns. Rome was occupied.

During the fighting in Piazza S. Maria Maggiore a priest was wounded and was carried into the Oriental Institute, which is directed by the Jesuits. Rumour went quickly round that "they" had shot a Jesuit.

By six everything was ominously quiet. Shops and houses were shut. There was no traffic except an occasional swiftly moving German car. People collected in little knots everywhere in the streets, dismayed, depressed, wondering almost in whispers what would happen next. Some had seen the fighting, some had stayed indoors for safety and had seen nothing. Each group had for centre one who professed to know what had really happened. Here and there the speaker was a bedraggled and hungry soldier, telling the tale of betrayal. His hearers made little comment. What was there to say? They had been tricked, and now the city was occupied. A nightmare had come true. What would it all mean? Anything was possible. Darkness fell and they went home dejectedly.

About seven o'clock we had news by telephone that an "agreement" had been made with the Germans, under the terms of which they were to remain outside Rome with the exception of three places only, which they would occupy. The places were: the German Embassy, the Roman broadcasting station, and the German telephone plant. They furthermore recognized Rome as an "open city," whatever that might mean. It all sounded better, and hope flickered up for a moment. Perhaps they might really retreat farther north; there isn't any particularly good line of defence near here, and they have already made two in the north, one from Ancona to Pistoia and the other on the Po. Yes, perhaps they would.

Again all night long we heard rifle shots in the streets.

Saturday September 11th

It was like a city of the dead. No shops open. No policemen about anywhere. No one going to work. No buses. No trams, or rather, the trams, a weird sight, were there motionless and empty, standing on their tracks exactly where they were yesterday when the siren sounded. Rome had been stunned and did not react. The shining exceptions to the general state of apathy were the bakers, who, out of sheer public spirit and on their own responsibility, opened up and made bread; somewhat late, but still by dinner time, there was the usual meagre ration of 150 grammes of bread for everyone. Those who had no provisions in reserve went hungry, for the looting of the Central Market and the closing of all the shops made food unprocurable all that day.

There were no street-cleaners with their brooms and hoses; and pathetic pools of blood lay on the pavement, blackening in the hot sunlight. The city was left to its own devices. During the morning, however, animosity roused itself and shooting began again in the streets. German soldiers who were sniped from windows retaliated with machine guns, particularly in Via Nazionale, Via del Tritone, again near the Ministry of the Interior and near the Station. Torn awnings, smashed brickwork, piles of loose plaster and broken glass testified to the violence of the clashes. More looting went on. Most people kept indoors.

At 1 o'clock the Roman radio, now German-controlled of course, broadcast the following:

Yesterday an armistice was agreed upon by the commanders of the German and Italian troops in the Roman area. Since then the behaviour of Italian soldiers has been such that the following measures have been taken:

1—It is forbidden to carry arms. Soldiers bearing them will be arrested and disarmed.

2—Anyone killing a German soldier will be shot. Otherwise the armistice remains in force.

So it was an armistice. Or wasn't it?

In the afternoon two newspapers appeared on single sheets: the *Giornale d'Italia* and the *Avvenire*. They carried a proclamation which repeated the conditions of the "armistice," and ordered all soldiers, of whatever rank, to report at their barracks within twenty-four hours, bringing their weapons with them and all civilians to deliver any firearms in their possession at the nearest police station immediately, and reminded them that obedience to the military authorities must be prompt and absolute. Court-martial would follow breaches of these orders. The document was signed "General Calvi di Bergolo," and was posted everywhere.

Calvi di Bergolo? Where was Caviglia? Caviglia, on whom we had placed our hopes—was he done away with already? And as for the Germans occupying only those three places in Rome—the German Embassy, the German telephone central and the Italian broadcasting station—well, it was just silly, as well as treacherous, to say so. The whole city was swarming with them. They were going about in armoured cars with machine guns pointed significantly at the passers-by, and on foot with revolvers and rifles—and a swaggering air. There were men from the air force, infantrymen, gunners, Afrika Korps, S.S. men and railway men too. German engine drivers had been hastily brought in because the commanders did not trust the Italian ones. And they were right, because nothing could please an Italian mechanic better than to drive his locomotive with a load of Germans behind it straight off the rails. They kept the Italian brakemen, however; but these had already made their plans. As soon as the Allies should be within striking distance of Rome there would no longer be any Italian brakemen on the trains; they would have vanished—only to reappear when the Allies would need their services. It was all nicely organized.

Calvi di Bergolo is the husband of Princess Yolanda of Savoy, eldest daughter of the King of Italy. He is a fine shot, an excellent horseman and a good cavalry officer, but a strong pro-

Nazi. It was obvious that he had been made responsible for order in Rome on account of his German sympathies. His picture appeared in the papers, three-quarter-face, looking back over his shoulder. "To hide his German decoration," was the general verdict. He had an infantry division at his command with which to keep order. The Germans had not gone to the length of putting their own men on police duty. But whoever might be in command or not in command, no police showed themselves today.

By evening there was another set of placards on the walls. The placards were making news. This one was even more arresting than Calvi di Bergolo's. It was signed "Feldmaresciallo Kesselring," and ran as follows:

1—The Italian territory under my command is declared to be war territory. It is subject throughout to German martial law.

2—Any crime committed in this territory against German armed forces will be punished according to German martial law.

3—Those organizing strikes or sabotage, as well as snipers, will be shot immediately.

4—Italian workers who will volunteer for German service will be treated according to German principles and will be paid according to the German scale of wages.

5—The Italian Ministers and Justices will remain in office.

6—Until further orders private correspondence is suspended. All telephone conversations should be as brief as possible, and they will be strictly supervised.

7—Italian civil authorities and organizations are responsible to me for the maintenance of public order. They will prevent all acts of sabotage and of passive resistance to German measures, and they will co-operate fully with the German organizations.

The curfew will continue to be at 9.30 P.M.

So that was that. It was well to know. No letters, incoming or outgoing, and they would listen in on our phone calls. No. 5 meant that no quislings had been put in office—yet. But probably it wouldn't be long before they were. There was also a notice in the papers to the effect that efforts were being made to bring food into the city; but the shops stayed shut and the Romans stayed hungry. An "agreement" and two proclamations in one day gave much food for thought, but none for the body.

In the preamble to his proclamation Calvi di Bergolo had

referred to Rome officially as an "open city." Perhaps it would keep us from being bombed, and again perhaps it wouldn't. How soon might the Allies be here, coming up from Cosenza, or making a landing somewhere? Conservative opinion said about two weeks. Could we manage to stick it out for all that time? There was no alternative.

We heard that Italian officers had already been arrested by the Germans and put in prison or in concentration camps. The men had been disarmed and told to go home until further orders. Army officers who had been arrested in Rome were offered their freedom on parole not to leave the city. It was perfectly clear what was afoot. How would it work? Life was apparently going to be punctuated with notes of interrogation.

Sunday September 12th

The day dawned hot and damp, with a white mist covering the city as if to stifle its angry dismay. It was one of those regular September mists like a fleecy blanket, above which emerged the dome of St. Peter's and the pylons of the broadcasting station symbolizing the fusion of old and new above the cloud, to bring about a happier future. But for us, the present was just chaos.

Last night Hitler made a wild "proclamation" saying that he had the whole of the Italian army in his hands; and that Italy would pay dearly for her base betrayal.

A plane or two drifted lazily across the sky, going nowhere in particular it would seem, but merely to show that they were there. They were German, of course.

By midday a few newspapers were on sale. They were interesting mainly for the blanks in their columns made by last-minute censorship. The *Popolo di Roma*, in the uncensored scraps of an editorial, spoke eloquent praise of the men in the street. It said:

Today, at last, the town authorities are moving. For four days we have witnessed an extraordinary phenomenon: that of the Roman people governing themselves, in the old classical sense of the verb "to govern." The feeling of civic responsibility has shown itself in inverse proportion to the eminence of the individuals. The more lowly the townsman and the more unofficial his character, the more initiative he showed. We

[11]

refer particularly to the bakers who baked, and the staffs of papers who published some news for the bewildered public. We say "some news" because its paucity was lamentable. The citizens of Rome have deserved well of their country.

For once, there was truth in what the *Popolo di Roma* said. A new proclamation by Calvi di Bergolo appeared in heavy type in a "box" on the front pages of the papers. It ran:

A MESSAGE TO THE ROMAN PEOPLE:

Romans, as commander of the open city of Rome, I hereby confirm my previous proclamation. Be calm and confident. The times through which we are passing are both serious and painful for all of us, but they might easily become more so, should your sense of responsibility and your patriotism waver. The authorities are doing all in their power to restore normal conditions in the city. I am dealing with the food problem. The public service will be regularly resumed. Each one of you should remain at his post and do his duty without unjustified anxiety.

People shrugged their shoulders. His intentions were good. It was a gesture. But did it mean anything? Mainly, it seemed to mean "Don't shoot the Germans." And that was just what they couldn't stop doing. Certainly there was some justification for it. In Via Veneto, in front of the Hotel Excelsior, a German tried to take a motor cycle away from an Italian soldier. The latter resisted, whereupon the German discharged his revolver into the petrol tank. The Italian fired at him and several other Italian and German soldiers having come up, the fight became general. It was stopped only by the arrival of some officers. Pedestrians fled down side streets as armoured cars rattled to the spot.

Monday September 13th

There were, if possible, even longer faces in the streets today than yesterday. Radio and newspapers proclaimed that Mussolini had been freed from prison by Hitler's parachutists. Anyone who thought, as the Germans did, that at the name of Mussolini Italy would rally again to the Fascist standard, ought to have

[12]

seen those faces. They showed not so much anger or resentment as plain disgust. Mussolini and his party were finished forever on July 25th, and no amount of galvanizing would raise the Fascist corpse to life. The whole thing is cordially hated. Yet there was some anxiety as to what violence might be encouraged by the Germans on the part of a few tough Fascists who had been hiding since July. They were ready to hand as willing instruments.

A few shops begin to open here and there; some food is on sale but not much. There are no police about. Rome is getting used to regulating its own traffic and keeping its own order, at least during the daytime. At night it is different. There was plenty of shooting in the streets last night, together with explosions of hand grenades.

The Germans are all over the town, and they have begun looting in earnest. They stop people in the street and take their jewels, rings, chains, watches and money from them at the muzzle of a revolver. They are also stealing bicycles and motor cars. They simply stop the cyclist or motorist, take the machine and leave the owner afoot. There is no redress. Their attitude is: "Well, and what are you going to do about it?" They alone are armed. It will be death for anyone else to be found with any weapons now, as there are orders for them to be given up to the authorities. The Germans surpassed themselves when they stopped Mgr. Rossignani (formerly secretary of the Pope when he was Cardinal Pacelli) and took the motor car he was driving. The Pope's physician, Dr. Galeazzi-Lisi, was wounded in the head by a German machine gun, when he was on his way to visit his patients. Duca Aquarone's magnificent villa was thoroughly looted last night; he is the Comptroller of the King's household and reputed to be one of the three (together with Grandi and Badoglio) who persuaded the King to have Mussolini arrested. He escaped with the King.

As a gesture toward keeping order, an Italian infantry regiment is camping in the Villa Borghese under the command of General Cappellini, but it seems to be more ornamental than useful.

G. came in this morning to warn us that a rumour is going round that 100 English people had been arrested and sent off to unknown destinations—it's ugly if it's true, but one never knows. The Germans are masters here, and can do what they like. A good many arrests will probably be made.

People are going back to work, by degrees. The trams and buses are running, heavily overloaded—possibly by the people whose cars and bicycles have been stolen.

The King and Badoglio are at Palermo, and the latter has directed the Italians, by radio, to join actively with the Allies in every way possible.

Yesterday St. Peter's was opened after remaining shut for two days. It was a relief for the Romans when they saw the big gates of the portico thrown back once more.

This morning a perfectly new type of khaki uniform appeared in the streets. The wearers carried Tommy guns, and wore tropical helmets. "The Americans are here!" The news ran through the city, and was even telephoned by friends. For the moment optimism was uppermost. But the matter was soon explained. The P.A.I. (Polizia Africa Italiana, Italian African Police), being a fine body of men highly trained and out of a job, had been called in to help in the policing of the city. Hope died again.

Tuesday September 14th

The days continue to be very hot. After a long spell of drought there still seems to be no hope of rain, and this long-drawn-out heat makes everything else more trying; it seems so unnecessary, in a way.

Last night the head of one of the great Roman families, famous for his charities and his uprightness, was attacked in his own palace. The fact that he never joined the Fascist party made him the object of their hatred. German soldiers, led by a Fascist, broke open the door of his apartment with the butts of their rifles and forced their way past the servant who tried to stop them. He and his family escaped through another door with only a few seconds leeway. In this case the German soldiers were genuine, in some others they have been Fascists disguised in German uniforms.

The situation all round is still very obscure. The press is gagged; pro-German editors have been appointed for all the papers. German commands have been established all over the city. They are also beginning to name new "commissioners" instead of the Ministers. M., who is on the staff at the Ministry for Foreign Affairs, went to his office in Palazzo Chigi as usual yesterday, and was met on the staircase by a squad of German soldiers who tried to arrest him, saying that the Ministry was occupied. He doubled back and escaped by a private staircase.

General Stahel is in command of the German forces in Rome; he is under Kesselring, who commands in "Central and Southern" Italy. Rommel commands in the North. Both Stahel's and Kesselring's signatures come out on the decrees which are continually posted on the walls of Rome. Some of these documents are printed both in German and in Italian. One wonders why. They apply only to Italians, who don't know German and wouldn't learn it if they were paid to do so.

The evening papers carry a statement of Stahel's saying that "Requisitions and sequestrations in the city of Rome"—not "open city" this time—"are only permitted on exhibition of a written document of authorization, signed by the German Command." Perhaps the rank and file overdid their highway robberies. The "Command" has, by now, taken practically every motor tire in Rome (when they have not taken the cars themselves) and all the bicycles they require, for the present.

Stahel has also issued another proclamation today stating that, after the armistice signed by Badoglio—followed by the usual vituperation of the latter—the German armed forces had assumed the protection of Italian soil, that "criminal elements" had opposed this action of theirs, but that "order being now re-established" the Italian authorities under General Calvi di Bergolo were henceforward responsible for the surrender of all weapons possessed by the people of Rome. "Therefore, after midnight on September 15th, anyone found in possession of arms will be shot." In concluding he remarked that "these disorders" had "imperilled innocent lives as well as the food supply of the city." Would he really cut off all food, if people continued to snipe Germans?

The Jews are in a panic, and trying to leave the city. They fear being sent to Germany as hostages. No one is safe. Nothing is certain. We might as well be back in the Dark Ages.

And down there ours are edging their way north of Salerno. Will they really be here in a few days?

Wednesday September 15th

The town is, on the whole, quieter, and there seems to be some hope of food, green vegetables, if nothing else, after a week without them. They say that the Germans are getting no supplies from the Vaterland and so must live on us. That being true, the outlook is fairly grim. Certainly they have looted enough food shops already, both officially and unofficially. Although this wholesale theft is in no way amusing, it has a funny side occasionally, or rather, the humourous aspect of it is provided by appalling stupidity in their efforts at propaganda. Yesterday they were taking photographs. German soldiers on a "commandeered" cart were distributing food, also "commandeered," to the crowd while a movie man made a reel of the scene. Farther on they gave a number of those big round country loaves of bread to some poor women, photographed them holding the loaves, then took back the bread and sent the women about their business.

Everyone is hiding whatever valuables can be hidden. Some bury theirs, others wall them up. When going out in the street they leave at home watches and anything else worth stealing. Women wear gloves over their rings, and men carry very little cash.

During the night numbers of the German proclamations on the walls were torn down under cover of darkness. As soldiers do not want to report at their barracks and civilians don't want to go to the police authorities to turn in their arms before midnight, weapons are being dropped about everywhere. A revolver and some cartridges turned up in our garden. A good many armoured cars are still cruising the streets.

In spite of the German domination here, neither shops nor banks will exchange German currency. Our dentist took care of a German with a bad toothache and was paid in marks. He went the rounds of the city to get them exchanged, but no one would look at them. Having failed everywhere, he won't accept marks again, toothache or no toothache.

[16]

The papers today give four columns of their poor single sheets to an effusion of Hitler's, the publication of which was "ordered by the German High Command of Southern Italy." Der Fuehrer spoke from his General Headquarters, and at his customary length, on the defection and the vileness of Italy, and on the entire course of the war. Among other things he said:

The loss of Italy has no real importance to us. For months the weight of the struggle there has been borne by us . . .

Perhaps he had in mind the way in which the Germans fired on the Italians in Sicily when they were being driven back by the Allies. He went on:

The attempt of international plutocracy to weaken German resistance is childish. . . . Their hopes of bringing about a collapse in Germany like that of July 25th in Italy spring from their fundamental error concerning my own personal position. . . . The German Government is more than ever fanatically united. . . . I am infinitely proud of being the leader of the German people and I thank God for every hour He grants me so that I may, by means of my own work, bring the greatest struggle in history to a victorious conclusion. The measures taken to safeguard German interests in Italy are very severe, but they have gone into effect and are now being carried out methodically. . . . The fate decreed for Italy should remind all countries that they should stand by their obligations to their allies. To the German people, now bearing this trial, Almighty God will, in the end, give the laurels of victory as a reward, and with these laurels the preservation of its own life.

The Ministers who were still in office have been removed today, and quisling "Commissioners" put in their places. They are all pro-German, of course. Nevertheless the son of the Commissar at the Ministero delle Comunicazioni, also pro-German, or at least he was such, who is an Italian officer, got locked up immediately after the armistice and is not out of prison yet. Numbers of Italian officers, especially in the neighbourhood of Rome, got locked up that way, just in case . . . The pro-Ally Italian officers have simply disappeared; that is to say they have gone into mufti, left their Roman residences and live, under assumed names, anywhere except where they would be identified. Rome offers plenty of hiding places for them;

after all, it is a place with a million and a half inhabitants, and you can't search every house every day, not even if you are an "S.S." or a Gestapo agent. Then they don't often stay in the same hideout for long; some of them move every night.

Thursday September 16th

Rome is quiet and sullen. The weather is very hot and the food situation is bad. Public opinion is pessimistic. The Germans are supposed to have mined the gas, water and electric plants, and intend blowing them all up before leaving. They apparently intend to blow up also several bridges, the Ministries of Foreign Affairs, of the Navy, of War and of Home Affairs, as well as some of the big hotels. We know what their destructions are like before they leave places; their policy is the famous "scorched earth," and they are adepts at carrying it out. At the same time they are enacting the farce of the "Open City" in all seriousness. When planes approach the siren does not sound; cars have appeared placarded with "Polizia—Roma Città Aperta," and the same words are printed on armlets worn by some soldiers and by the regular police.

Optimists are saying that the Germans will be taken by surprise by the quick arrival of the Allies, and will have to leave Rome in such haste that they won't have time to blow things up. Or else they argue that as the Germans have got everything they wanted, that is, practically all the motors, motor tires and petrol that Rome has to offer, they will depart northward to hold the line of the Po, or perhaps the "Arezzo line" in Tuscany. They add, in confirmation of their opinions, that German trucks and motorized units have been leaving Rome going northward by the Via Flaminia. Of course the pessimists reply: "Oh yes? And how many more were coming in from the south by the Via Appia as your lot was leaving by the Flaminia?" Numbers of stray soldiers are wandering about still. Officers have been told that if they reside in Rome they are to go to their houses, give their word of honour not to leave the city, and report daily at headquarters. Each time they did report, of course they would be asked if they would volunteer for the German army, and each time they would say "No." In the long run they would probably be arrested and sent to a concentration camp, so they prefer not to pledge themselves by any word of honour, and simply to vanish.

The "suicide" of Marshal Cavallero was announced this morning. A man of 62, of great military ability, he was one of the finest officers in the Italian army. He had been in contact with Badoglio before the fall of Mussolini on July 25th, and was anxious to save Italy from the abyss toward which Fascism was driving her. The Germans arrested him after the armistice. The official statement says "He was freed from arrest, but unable to bear his country's dishonour he put an end to his own life." The truth is that the Germans sent for him, and explained that they wanted his help in forcibly raising recruits for them, and in other jobs of the same type. He knew what was coming, and said to his wife, as he left his house to go to the German headquarters: "I don't think that I shall come back from there." To the Germans' astonishment he refused their demands. As he now knew too much about their intentions and methods, there was, for them, only one way out of the difficulty, so they shot him then and there. In spite of the fulsome praise in the press notice of his "suicide," the truth was known. The German authorities summoned his wife at once, and with many expressions of sympathy showed her the body with the right hand still raised as if in the act of firing a revolver. She stood there for a moment, then said quietly: "You forget, gentlemen, that my husband was left-handed."

More restrictive measures appeared today. All permits to be about after the curfew have been cancelled; they had previously been given to priests, doctors, nurses and journalists. Police headquarters are established at the Ministry of War, and no permission is given to keep even sporting guns or ammunition.

The Vatican City is "protected" by German troops, although they have made no attempt to occupy it. The idea seems to be that they are "protecting" it from the Allies. Two German paratroopers slouch in a dispirited manner near the colonnade of St. Peter's, carrying Tommy guns. They wear battle dress, that is helmets resembling tortoise-shell basins in colour and design, and short green-and-brown-streaked camouflage overalls on top of their summer uniforms of buff cotton. In bearing and outline they suggest penguins. Sometimes they stand in the colonnade, out of the hot sun, but they never go inside the white line which marks the boundary of the Vatican City. In fact, whether on or off duty they are forbidden to enter it. Inside the Vatican City serious police measures have been taken and the commanders of the Vatican forces are very much on the qui vive. A large number of extra Palatine Guards have been taken on, the numbers of Swiss Guards and Gendarmes on duty have been doubled, and ten Noble Guards are on the watch night and day outside the Pope's private apartments. Many of the latter who lived in Rome have taken up their quarters in the Vatican so as to be within call.

Naturally, if the Germans chose to occupy the Vatican City by force, the Pontifical guards would be powerless, and these new measures are taken mainly to prevent any sudden inrush of a mob. It is quite possible that, if panic-stricken by some action on the part of the Germans, the Romans might surge into the Vatican for protection. The Swiss carry rifles now instead of pikes, but they would never fire on a crowd of that kind; all they could do would be to close the gates and hold them. Extra gates have been added where convenient and all the entrances are sedulously watched. Those having business there must present credentials and receive a special pass before they are allowed in. Fortunately my Vatican Library reader's identity card is acceptable to the plain-clothes police agent who issues the passes. Of course spies of every shade and colour could easily make the little Vatican City their happy hunting ground unless precautions were taken. As a matter of fact the Library is closed, although one may keep one's card of admission for future use. There was a good deal too much talking in the Library lobby and courtyard, and a few spies and "agents provocateurs" did make their way in there under pretence of study. There might have been serious trouble had not both the spies and the imprudent talkers been firmly excluded.

Even to enter St. Peter's, lay folk have to show some sort of identification card; that is to say, when it is open. Sometimes they shut it altogether. Yesterday a German truck pulled up near the colonnade, having brought food for the paratroop sentinels; a tripod was erected on it, bearing a powerful telescope, and through it, all comings and goings at the Vatican City were observed. Today the sentinels are not there, bored probably by the prosaic happenings they sighted during their vigil.

Certainly the Germans, whatever their motive may be, are trying to make friends with the Vatican. Their Ambassador to the Holy See, Baron von Weiszacker, is extremely courteous and shows every consideration to the Pope. There has been no looting in churches or religious houses, and apologies were made for stealing Mgr. Rossignani's car. Probably, when their inevitable *débâcle* comes, they want to have friends at the Vatican to salvage what may be salvaged. The atmosphere inside the Vatican City is one of great peace and calm. I was struck this morning by its apparent remoteness from the struggle. It was also very pleasant not to see German uniforms about. The Pontifical postal facilities are cut off, but the broadcasting station, one of the most powerful in Europe, is functioning, and there is no interference with it. Shortly before his death Marconi personally supervised its installation, and it is of inestimable value at the present moment. Motors with the regular "S.C.V." Vatican City license plates pass freely in Rome, and all the "extraterritorial" Vatican premises there are unmolested. They all have a placard posted on their doors bearing the words "Property of the Holy See" both in Italian and in German. Cardinals Massimi and Pizzardo have left their usual residences and have gone to live in the Vatican City, as have some of the Jesuits connected with the radio station. It is simpler to do so, and avoids complications. The Palatine Guard will take over the policing of the Lateran Palace and of the Pontifical property at Castel Gandolfo. Food and provisions of all kinds come straight into the Vatican City by their own railway line, and thus the authorities can feed their own "citizens" and give a helping hand to some of the religious houses in Rome. But of course they cannot achieve the impossible, and, as some people think they do, feed all the convents and monasteries in Rome.

Today Mussolini, from his secret residence in the north of Italy, has issued "Orders of the Day," re-establishing Fascism, naming it "The Republican Fascist Party," directing all officials to resume the positions from which they were ousted by the Badoglio government, giving orders to "help the people," to punish traitors and, above all, to support the Germans in Italy. The wording of these messages is unlike his style, so it looks as if he were either dead, or so ill that he is nothing but a figurehead useful to the Germans.

The last placard on the walls today prohibits meetings of every kind, under the usual severe penalties. It is signed by General Stahel, who, by the way, is a very decent man, an Austrian and a Catholic. Perhaps it is part of their policy toward the Holy See to have put him here. He is supposed not to see eye to eye with Kesselring, who is in command of "Central and Southern Italy."

This afternoon Mrs. Arthur Strong died in a nursing home in Via Mecenate. She was certainly the most learned woman archaeologist of our day. She was a C.B.E.; M.A. Cambridge; Life Fellow of Girton; Litt.D. Dublin; Hon. LL.D., St. Andrews; Hon. Litt.D., Manchester; Fellow of the Society of Antiquaries; Fellow of the Scottish Society of Antiquaries; Vice-President of the Hellenic Society; Hon. Member of the Archaeological Society of Athens; Hon. Member of the Archaeological Institute of America; Member of the Pontifical Roman Academy; of the Società Italiana di Storia Patria; Foreign Member of the Reale Accademia dei Lincei and of the Reale Accademia di S. Luca; Member of the Arcadian Academy and of the Accademia dei Virtuosi del Panteone. From 1909 until 1925 she was Assistant Director of the British School at Rome. From that period until the outbreak of the war her flat in Via Balbo was the meeting place of intellectuals, students, littérateurs and diplomats of every country, drawn to Rome as by a magnet; but particularly English and Italian scholars met there. Her masterly work on "Roman Sculpture" was followed by other books, treatises and articles in English, French and Italian, and she was at work on a history of the architectural development of the Vatican Palace when death took her. One of her last utterances was: "My book!" The loss to British scholarship is irreparable. Her friends were consoled by the thought that for the last eight days of her life she had been unconscious, and never knew that the Rome she loved so well was occupied by the Huns. She was buried according to her wish in the habit of a Dominican Tertiary, and rarely have I seen a more fitting framework for a noble face and form than those austere folds of black and white. She was buried in the Anglo-Saxon plot in the "Veran Field," Campo Verano—the cemetery where, not quite two thousand years ago, St. Lawrence was buried by the Christian matron Lucina. The place still shows signs of the devastation wrought by the bombing of July 19th, and numbers of coffins are lying about awaiting re-interment; fortunately the Anglo-Saxon plot of ground was not damaged.

Friday September 17th

Our men are fighting their way through at Salerno, and there is no sign of a landing in these parts. Well, it's only a week since the Battle of Rome and the occupation, and one mustn't get impatient.

Unofficial looting has decreased. Shops and warehouses that had anything left in them are being emptied systematically, but private soldiers don't rob you in the streets any more.

Another "Order of the Day" signed by Mussolini appoints Renato Ricci commander in chief of the Milizia Volontaria di Sicurezza Nazionale, which is to Fascism what the S.S. men are to Nazism. Pavolini, one of the Fascist Ministers, says in a foolish speech made today that Fascism is coming into its own again. Everyone believes that Mussolini is dead and that the whole thing is a put-up job.

Arms and hand grenades are scattered about disconcertingly, just where their owners dropped them instead of returning them to the military stores. Children pick them up and play ball with them, but not for long. They burst, and the players are killed or wounded. In the suburbs a cow swallowed a small one that was lying in the long grass, and of course the poor animal exploded.

Last night we heard loud detonations in the distance, and thought it must mean a landing at Ostia or Prática di Mare. It turned out afterward that someone had placed a bomb under the barracks of the Fascist militia and had succeeded in blowing them up.

This is our tenth day without milk. The Germans have commandeered the cows in the neighbourhood. Some green vegetables are coming in, but very few, on account of the lack of transport facilities.

Notices in the press and posters on the walls direct all soldiers from the class of 1885 to that of 1905 to report at headquarters. But they're all in hiding, and no one turns up. Calvi di Bergolo has published orders to hand over all motor cars which have not received a special license, and the Germans have begun to search garages for them. It is hard to hide them successfully, yet some owners have achieved it.

Saturday September 18th

Terrific explosions last night. Were they the Littorio airfield? The Centocelle one? The Ciampino one? All are quite close to us. Or were the Allies bombing one of those endless German columns that are always coming and going on the roads near Rome? Travel of any sort is definitely unhealthy at present. Of the few trains that start, many are either bombed or machine-gunned before they arrive. Lorries meet the same fate, however much they are camouflaged with grass nets.

This afternoon there was good news from Salerno. They seem to be out of the woods, but, judging from the British radio, it was touch-and-go there for a while. Everyone hangs on the B.B.C. reports, which are broadcast almost continuously in Italian, English, French and other European languages. This infuriates the Germans. Orders are published and penalties threatened, reports are printed of people fined and imprisoned for listening to "enemy broadcasts," but they have no effect whatever. Outside aerials are banned and everything is done to stop the listening, short of searching all houses and confiscating every radio.

Sunday September 19th

Mussolini spoke on the German-controlled Italian radio last night. It did not sound like his voice and it was not his style. The Roman populace immediately said: "*47, morto che parla.*" They all gamble in the public lotteries and buy the book of omens which assigns numbers to everything seen or dreamt of.

Now in that book if a dead man speaks to you in your dream, it means that you must gamble on number 47. So they went and staked their lire on the fateful number.

Twenty-three Germans were murdered at Monte Mário last night. Resentment against them is growing. "They are starving us," say the people, "and they ought to be killed." On account of these murders the officials at the German Embassy, where they have taken in a large number of extra officers and clerks over and above their usual staff, seem to be growing nervous. A severe ordinance came out today forbidding anyone to pass along the streets which bound the house and garden during curfew hours, that is from 9.30 P.M. to 4.30 A.M. Not even persons living in those streets may go in or out. The Embassy occupies what is known as the Villa Wolkonsky, a princely house with a wonderful garden near St. John Lateran. The neighbourhood is policed by German soldiers with guns.

Monday September 20th

Kesselring was received by the Pope yesterday *"in forma privatissima."* They say he is a good Catholic. What passed? Not the best of the "best-informed" will ever be able to tell us. But there is the fact, and that's enough for twenty hopes and fears. Possibly it had something to do with the paragraph which appeared afterward in the official Vatican newspaper, the *Osservatore Romano*. It ran as follows:

Many rumours have been spread regarding conditions in the Vatican City and the person of the Holy Father, since the German occupation of Rome. As we have already stated, from the afternoon of September 13th, German soldiers have been posted in Piazza San Pietro, in Italian territory, outside the boundaries of the Vatican City. This action was preceded by a telephone call from the Italian Command of the City of Rome to the Governor of the Vatican City, who gave notice to the authorities. Two Vatican officials were directed to present themselves at the time appointed, 4 P.M., at the boundary line of the Vatican City to make sure that the territory of the neutral Pontifical State was respected. These officials verified the fact that the said boundary line had not been transgressed.

The Vatican officials referred to were the commanders of the Swiss Guard and the Palatine Guard.

Strong articles appeared in the press against those who "fail to collaborate with the German forces," especially by murdering them, is implied.

Forced labour was instituted here today. Men from 23 to 28 are mobilized "for important work needed by the German Command and for provisioning the city of Rome." In other words they are to mend roads and bridges for the Germans, dig trenches, build fortifications and lay railway tracks for them. They count on getting from the city of Rome alone about 6,000 young men. Those who do not report will be court-martialled. "Volunteers" are also asked for among men outside the given age groups. They graciously "suspend military service" for those mobilized for labour. Boys from 18 to 22 are also called up for military service today. So run the placards.

The sentinels on duty at night in the streets surrounding the German Embassy have orders to fire without warning on anyone approaching from any direction. Last night one of them, rather the worse for drink, saw figures on an adjacent roof, seemingly beckoning to each other. Outlined against the sky they provided easy targets. He fired, with no result. He fired again. Again no result. A platoon rushed to the spot and identified the "beckoning" men as the stone figures of Saints which surmount the façade of St. John Lateran.

Tuesday September 21st

The German High Command ordains that black market practitioners shall be punished by death, or by imprisonment for lesser offences in that line. They also order that the *portoni* of all houses must be closed by 8 P.M. They don't want to run the risk of people leaping out on them in the dark, and rushing indoors for refuge.

More and more people are hiding, moving their lodgings or taking to the hills. It is still warm and mild, and the Allies are expected here shortly—but suppose they delay? The people in the hills will die of hunger and exposure. You are considered a pessimist if you think that the Allies will not be here until the middle of October. If only they could make it. . . .

Our plumber has been here, crying quite openly. His only son, a boy of 18, was called up in July and reported for military service. He was sent to Cremona with some others from Rome. After the armistice, they realized that they would have to fight for the Germans, and planned to escape. His mother, receiving no news at all, went to Cremona to investigate. There were no signs of Antonio, but the people there told her that six boys from Rome had tried to get away through a drain that ran underneath a cemetery. When the Germans got wind of it, they walled up both ends of the drain, with the boys inside. Their only ray of hope is that their boy may not have been one of the six. No one can tell them.

There is a persistent rumour that Franco has told the Germans that if they do anything to the Pope, he will open Spain to the Allies. It doesn't seem likely, but there may be something in it.

We are burying our valuables, having a nice little garden which affords scope for such activities. We buried them darkly after supper, aided by a small electric torch until somebody said: "Douse the glim," for fear of neighbours watching us. They're in a tin box, wrapped in oilcloth, so perhaps they won't be ruined by the rain when it comes. It was quite Stevensonian and romantic, in spite of the sound of German army boots in the street outside.

Mussolini has constituted his Ministry, the names are published today. Graziani is Minister for Defence. People are horrified, for Graziani is a great soldier, though a butcher by reputation; it seems impossible that such a man should have put himself at the service of such a gang. Was it just for a handful of silver, or on account of his long-standing rivalry with Badoglio? Possibly this was his weak spot. His mental powers are supposed to be somewhat erratic. Those who defend him say that probably he was, like Cavallero, threatened with a revolver and gave in. But Cavallero went on refusing and died.

All men born in 1921, '22, '23, '24 and '25 are called up for "labour service," which means that they will either be taken to Germany or be put to building and repairing roads and digging trenches for the Germans in Italy; they are to present themselves at the Labour Office at once. Of course, no one intends to do so.

The Germans are also trying desperately to get volunteers for their army among Italians, particularly specialized workmen, such as mechanics, interpreters, electricians, tailors, shoemakers, cooks. They have not yet grasped the fact that everyone is hiding from them, although they offer "privileges," good food, lodging and pay. The posters are ridiculous in their solemn stupidity; some are just proclamations, some are coloured drawings; one of the latter shows a group of brutalized-looking workers, smiling helplessly, like tame orangoutangs. The posters come straight from Germany, and one recognizes the work of a man who has already provided Italy with other equally repulsive drawings, especially on the outbreak of war. They are naïvely meant to work up enthusiasm. If the Germans would only look at the faces of the Italians when they see these efforts at persuasion . . . A long printed proclamation by Kesselring, appearing today, points out to all Italian officers that their oath of loyalty to the King of Italy is no longer valid, and that, as men of honour, they must now join the German forces or take a command in the "labour service." No one dares laugh openly at these proclamations, but under cover of darkness many of them are torn and defaced. The other day I walked behind a woman who carried a bunch of keys in her hand, and all the way down Via Boncompagni, as far as the Hotel Excelsior, where Germans are lodging, she ran those keys across a new set of posters, still wet with paste. I expected her arrest every moment, but nothing happened.

The Fascists are coming forward in the pose of saviours of the people, saying that they are "the buffer between the Germans and the populace." They have re-established the headquarters of their Roman group, the Fascio Romano, at Palazzo Braschi, where they used to be before their fall from power on July 25th. It is a very handsome building, erected by Pope Pius VI of the House of Braschi, situated on Corso Vittorio Emanuele, near Piazza Navona. It now contains offices for "social relief," for enlistments and for all Party activities. The black pennons of the Fascists have been hung from the balcony, together with the Roman standard and the Italian flag, but the latter has been stripped of the royal coat of arms in the centre. Some truculent-looking youths with black shirts and rifles were lounging in the doorway today when I passed there, and the bunting was all hanging down disconsolately in the September drizzle. The press says: "The old Fascist offices are in full activity, combatants, Party members and the Roman people are flocking to them." There was very little flocking this morning.

Saturday September 25th

Graziani spoke today on the radio, and if people were disgusted when they heard that he had taken command of the Fascist forces, they were nauseated by what he said. The speech was one long tirade against Badoglio's person. He called him a coward, a liar, a traitor, a deserter, a slave driver, blamed him for the Italian reverses in the present war, and referred to Caporetto in the last war. Of the many undignified public speeches that have been made since 1939, this was the most undignified. After all there are limits to the washing of dirty linen in public. Poor Graziani.

Calvi di Bergolo has been arrested and deported to Germany. He refused to give up 3,000 hostages for the labour service when the Germans ordered him to do so; his wife, Princess Yolanda, is with the rest of the women of the royal family in Switzerland. General Presti has been appointed to command the police of Rome, so the Germans are policing us in all but name.

The Swedes, the Spaniards and the Swiss are in a slightly difficult position at present, as their governments do not recognize the Fascist Republic. "Pinocchio's Republic" is its popular name. The Swiss Minister could not get his passport in order to consult with the authorities at Berne. It is a good thing he is not leaving, for the Swiss are now taking care of the diplomatic interests of twenty-five countries. Here in Italy, stranded foreigners owe them an unbounded debt of gratitude. Their efforts to help and to make conditions easier for those who are in trouble are as unfailing as their courtesy and consideration. When the war is over, the merits of these Swiss functionaries should be made known throughout the world.

Sunday September 26th

Private looting continues mildly; official looting, the regular searching of premises, continues steadily. This is what happens in the milder way. A party of Germans will go to a restaurant, eat and drink heartily, and when the bill is presented will tear it up saying: "Badoglio pays for this."

The Pope has discontinued all public audiences, those long ones which lasted from 9.30 A.M. until 1.30 P.M., in the course of which people of every kind and degree used to come to get his blessing. This is not the moment for crowds to assemble, and even if it were desirable there would be no means of doing so as the buses are fewer and fewer, and the trams are hopelessly crowded. They are indescribable. I have seen people trying to get in by the windows.

Monday September 27th

Kesselring's decree of today concerns motor vehicles. All those who possess them are to bring them to the Macao barracks, if not they will be severely punished. It is added that they will be paid for according to German valuation. This order includes not only private cars, but lorries, taxis, and a given number of motor buses. For a city of more than 1,500,000 inhabitants, this is going to make things almost impossible. Bicycles cannot be bought, and the Germans have already stolen numbers of them. The requisitioning of lorries will make the food question more acute than ever; supplies are already very low, as it is.

The Fascists have begun changing the names of streets. Piazza Montecitorio (the old *Mons Accettorius* of the Roman Republic) is to be Piazza Ettore Muti, in honor of one of their heroes who was killed in a fight with the police. Corso Umberto is to be Corso del Popolo, and Corso Vittorio Emanuele is to be Corso della Costituente. But no one pays any attention to them, and the old names cling. The royal coat of arms on the letter boxes has been painted out with black. The Fascist Republic is making an effort to imitate the doings of July 25th, when their emblems were torn down all over Rome, in the first fine careless rapture of the people on the fall of Mussolini. It is a very feeble imitation indeed, for then it was a joyous riot or popular enthusiasm, now it is a half-hearted daubing of black paint here and there on the Cross of Savoy.

More orders have been published, with added emphasis, that those called up for labour service MUST present themselves at once. So far, out of the 3,000 who should have joined up in the city of Rome, 60 have put in an appearance.

It is reported that Calvi di Bergolo wrote to his wife saying that, whatever happened, she might be sure that he would never commit suicide.

Tuesday September 28th

They're at the Jews. One wondered when it would come. Yesterday, the German authorities sent for the Chief Rabbi and told him that unless by midday today the Jews delivered one million lire and fifty kilogrammes of gold, some of them would be deported and others shot. It was a terrible moment, but they managed it. At the very last, they appealed to the Pope, who helped them to complete the amount. Now that they have paid their ransom, the Rabbi ought to destroy his register of Jewish residents in Rome. Although the Germans said that on condition of this payment they would leave them alone, how can they be trusted? The Romans are shocked and depressed; now that this sort of Jew-baiting has begun it has come home to them that they are really under the heel of the enemy.

Wednesday September 29th

The Fascist Republican Government announces that it has been functioning as from September 27th, and that it will shortly summon a Constituent Assembly to decide on details of its organization.

Kesselring's proclamation of today is unusually remarkable.

It is a development of his generalized appeal last Friday, to urge Italian officers to join the German army. This one says:

> The enemy has, for the time being, taken possession of Italian soil, and he must be driven out. *It is imperative to reassemble the disbanded Italian troops, in order that they may continue the war in the ranks of the German army.* . . . Those who enlist will have the same rights and therefore the same duties as German officers and soldiers.

All the Roman papers carried this proclamation. The Italians simply loathe the Germans, but the latter do not seem to have grasped the fact. German brutality to Italian soldiers when retreating in Russia and in Tunisia will never be forgotten in Italy, apart from their resentment on account of the Germans cutting down the Roman food supply while themselves living on what is left of the fat of the land.

Thursday September 30th

Even Graziani saw that Kesselring had overshot the mark, and urged him to withdraw his proclamation. So the Roman papers published today in heavy type: "Suspension of the proclamation regarding enlistment of Italian soldiers.—Marshal Graziani, Minister of National Defence, in agreement with General Stahel, German Commander of Rome, announces that the statement of the German Command concerning the enlistment of Italian soldiers, as published in the Roman press yesterday, is suspended."

On the other hand, Kesselring indulges in a whole column of persuasion for Italian workers to go to Germany, with alluring promises of pay and prosperity, and pointing out that "they will thus contribute materially to the final victory and to the future of a better Europe." Just that. The appeal is reinforced by lurid posters of sleek workers with suitcases walking toward a horizon bounded by an enormous eagle and a swastika.

Friday October 1st

One of our friends has a villa at Grottaferrata. He went out to see what was happening there, and found the Germans in possession. They told him blithely that they had selected it because it was heated, and they would be there for the winter. They had stolen most of the things he had left in the house, and shot up a good many cupboards which they wanted to open. But for the winter? We are already battering at the suburbs of Naples and Foggia. Naples is only three hundred kilometres from Rome, and an army can advance at the rate of ten kilometres a day if all goes well. Must we wait the whole winter? Surely not.

Saturday October 2nd

The Germans are taking up the railroad tracks on the lines they do not want to use, and are sending them to Germany.

Naples is taken. Thank God.

Sunday October 3rd

We are constantly asked to suggest possible hiding places for men who are trying to escape from military and labour service with the Germans. Everybody seems to be hiding. Some of the Germans are deserting and trying to hide also; they are mainly Austrians. The common soldiers are sick and tired of the war, but not the officers. If you get into conversation with the former they make no bones about saying that five years of fighting is too much of a good thing, and that they want to get back to see their families. They are having practically no mail here in Italy, and that makes it worse for them. Not all Hitler's toughening can desentimentalize them.

Monday October 4th

We are now receiving directions through the press and the radio to accumulate supplies of drinking water, with minute instructions how to sterilize and preserve it. The Germans are expected to blow up the water supply plant when they leave Rome. If they also blow up the electric plant we shall have to grope about in the dark and go to bed at dusk, because candles are unprocurable and there is no kerosene or petrol; they disappeared long ago.

There is talk too of a "state of emergency" which will be announced by the ringing of the church bells and the sound of sirens. During it no one will be allowed out of doors. It would probably precede the Germans' withdrawal, and they would be enabled to rifle houses, deport men, do whatever they chose, and depart without being disturbed by the populace.

Tuesday October 5th

Foggia is taken—at last. Now we can use those airfields for the Balkans. We shall get much less wheat up here, of course, as the plains round Foggia were the granary of Italy. It is not a pleasant prospect, because the food supplies are quite low enough already.

The Fascist Republican Party published a manifesto today in which they said that they would punish traitors severely, and could have no mercy on those who had made Fascists suffer during the 45 days following July 25th. They are nothing if not violent.

Wednesday October 6th

More preparations for the "emergency days." Bakers are to supply their clients with enough "biscuit bread" to last three days. It is ordinary bread sliced and dried in the oven, and is to be kept carefully until the moment comes when it will be urgently needed.

This morning the King's bodyguard, those superb six-foot *Corazzieri,* were arrested and taken away, just as, in the same way, the *Carabinieri* were disarmed and removed from their barracks in lorries.

The Queen's ladies-in-waiting and the Roman aristocracy generally seem to have aroused the anger of the Germans, or rather, that of the Fascists; the Germans probably don't mind so much, only of course they have to back the Fascists. Today they tried to arrest Princess Colonna. A plain-clothes policeman called at the Colonna Palace and told her that she was under arrest and must go with him. She asked if she might get her hat and coat and left him sitting there, escaping from the palace by another door. After some time, Prince Colonna came in casually and asked the man what he wanted. When he said he was waiting

[34]

for the Princess, Prince Colonna answered that she was not in the palace and he had no idea where she was. In retaliation, he has been placed under house arrest. Fortunately it is a big building with fine gardens, so he has plenty of room for ranging about.

Friday October 8th

The belated autumn rains have set in, the Tiber is rising, and with it, the southern rivers like the Volturno must be rising too. The Pope received the German Ambassador to the Holy See today. Optimists suggest that it is a good sign.

Saturday October 9th

Man-hunting has begun. The Germans placed sentries with machine guns on some of the bridges this morning, and cordons cutting off some of the streets in the Prati quarter then rounded up all the men they found inside the enclosure. They were put in lorries and taken away; no one knows whether they were for Germany, for work on the roads in Italy, or for prison as hostages.

Sunday October 10th

Every parish priest in Rome today told his congregation that the Pope had summoned them recently and had said that they were to urge their parishioners to be calm and self-possessed in whatever circumstances they might find themselves; to point out that self-control and moderation were needed above all in times like these, and to say that he relied on them to take this advice to heart and to act upon it. This was necessary because word has come through regarding the way the Italians behaved when the Germans left Naples, firing on them, and throwing boiling water and missiles of every kind down on them from the windows. There is even a story that the owner of a flat, finding nothing else heavy enough to hand, dropped a piano from the second floor. This was the sort of thing that caused such terrible reprisals in Naples.

Yesterday Villa Savoia, the King's private residence, was looted, officially and thoroughly. Furniture, paintings, statues, carvings, marbles, bronzes, tapestries, silver, bedding, linen, private belongings of the royal family, everything went, including the nails in the walls. The Quirinal has not been touched, being ranked as "national property."

Monday October 11th

There is something very obscure about the whole situation here. In Piazza Colonna, where the Fascists have reoccupied the central building ornamented with the famous portico from Veii, there are tanks, machine guns and young Blackshirt swashbucklers lounging about ostentatiously.

Having polished off Villa Savoia yesterday, the Germans are looting the pawnshops today, taking the wretched little belongings of the poor as well as the more valuable stuff.

Tuesday October 12th

The recent landing at Termoli was a splendid achievement. If only they can go ahead, take Chieti and Pescara, they can come on to Rome by way of Avezzano and Tivoli. It would be a pincer movement from the Adriatic and the Tyrrhenian. The Romans are getting depressed. "But do they know what it is like in Rome? Why don't they hurry up and get here? Why don't they land all over the place as well as at Termoli and finish it off quickly?" In their anxiety they are like children. We are miserable and anxious too, but we cling to the sheet-anchor conviction that the Allies know what they're doing, and that there are bigger issues at stake than Rome—and us.

We hear that the Appian Way has been blown up from Capua to Velletri.

Wednesday October 13th

The German Command is angry. In Torpignattara, one of the slum suburbs, where their lorries pass continually, people took to throwing little triangular spikes in the road; they are about two

inches long, and however they fall, there is always one point
uppermost. The effect on motor tires may be imagined. Several
unfortunate locksmiths who live in the neighbourhood were
arrested and the Germans threaten reprisals on the whole quarter if more of these spikes appear.

Thursday October 14th

They're angry again. Telephone wires have been cut, particularly some that were essential to them. They are not able to
identify the cutter, so they threaten to punish everyone who
lives near the spot.

Friday October 15th

In the Vatican the Palatine Guard is being considerably enlarged. This is necessary, because the other pontifical armed forces
cannot be increased, and more guards are needed in the Vatican
City and in all the extraterritorial pontifical property throughout
Rome and at Castel Gandolfo. There have been sixteen thousand
applications, for it is a heaven-sent opportunity of escaping from
Rome into the Vatican City, where there will be no man-hunting. But only 2,500 can be accepted. Their uniform was not
particularly attractive, as it had been unaltered since 1870, with
a peaked French shako piped with magenta. However they have
changed all that, and a dashing magenta béret is worn, very wide
and floppy, caught up with the pontifical cockade of yellow and
white, and instead of a stiff coat they wear a swirling military
cloak of dark blue. One does see some of them with civilian
trousers beneath this glory, but you can't have everything with
the present shortage of materials. They also carry rifles and ammunition.

Two thousand Gestapo and S.S. men have arrived to spy on
the German soldiers in case they are not behaving as Himmler
would wish, to carry out the dirty work connected with the
Jews, and to make themselves generally useful. So now, we have
here three groups of German authorities, quite independent of
one another: first, the German Embassy to the Holy See, headed
by Baron von Weiszacker; second, the German Military Com-

mand under General Stahel; third, the Gestapo and the S.S. men exclusively subject to Himmler. A number of the latter are lodged at the big Pensione Sta. Caterina in Corso d'Italia.

Saturday October 16th

"Writing on the wall" is showing itself here with a vengeance. Overnight hundreds of inscriptions in red paint appeared in praise of communism, of Russia and of Stalin. *Viva la Russia! Viva Stalin! Viva il Communismo! Abasso i Tedeschi! Abasso Mussolini! Abasso il Fascismo!* with the Hammer and Sickle accompanying them. They were everywhere, in the Trastevere, in the shopping quarters, in the expensive residential quarters, and, most conspicuous of all, in huge letters on the steep wall of the Tiber embankment. The wide sweep of the Trinità steps did not escape, for they appeared across Cardinal de Polignac's commemorative inscription in the centre of the terrace landing. The Fascist police fell over themselves trying to obliterate them, and daubs of grey paint hide the lettering, but proclaim loudly what is underneath. A policeman rang our bell one day and said in a hoarse whisper: "Have you seen what is on your wall?" Forgetting about the possibilities of inscription I said "No, whatever is it?" Sinking his voice still lower he said, "The Hammer and Sickle." Together we went out and inspected a small Hammer and Sickle in chalk. "Have you any whitewash?" he whispered, still in awed tones. When I said no, he quite contentedly said that he would get a friend to attend to the matter, and went off. Anyway, he didn't blame us; in fact he was rather by way of sympathizing with us for having such a terrible thing happen to our wall.

Sunday October 17th

The S.S. are doing exactly what one expected, and at 4.30 A.M. began to round up the Jews in their own houses. The Rabbi did not destroy his registers, and they know where every Jew lives. And this, after the promise made when they produced that ransom. . . . Some Jews escaped, others were herded into open lorries in the rain, and we know nothing about their destination.

[38]

It is a nameless horror. People you know and esteem, brave, kind, upright people, just because they have Jewish blood, treated like this. Some of them are heroic. They came for the father of a family we know. He was out. The Germans said in that case they would take his wife. Whereupon the daughter said: "Where my mother goes, I go too"—and although they did not want her particularly, she was taken as well.

Monday October 18th

The Leaflet Bogey stalks through Rome. Our Teutonic masters have a deadly fear of leaflets, of unkind remarks, of critical words. There is simply no end to their childishness in some cases, as there is none to their brutality in others. Here is a warning published today:

In the letter boxes of various apartment houses there have been found leaflets calculated to spread alarm and to give a bad impression of the German authorities. They were slipped in with the knowledge and consent of the porters. While we condemn the absolute untruth of the statements in these leaflets, we warn porters that under the Civilian Mobilization Act they are subject to military law. Should such leaflets be distributed again, the porters will be arrested and sent to a concentration camp. Private citizens are reminded that if they should find any of these leaflets it is their duty to inform the police of the Open City of Rome immediately. Those who do not do so will be held responsible in the same way as the porters and will be reported immediately to the military tribunal."

Oh, why didn't we get one? We've been cheated of a fine souvenir.

Tuesday October 19th

It is understood that the Pope has asked the German Ambassador to make an effort to help the Jews. It is difficult for von Weiszacker, of course, as the S.S. are independent of him. However, he did have some measure of success, for we hear that the women and children will be released.

Numbers of shops are boarding up their windows to save the glass from German or Fascist exuberance in street fighting, also to discourage looting. Others, not content with boarding, are bricking up both windows and doors and finishing them off with a coat of plaster. It gives the city a sinister look; while the presence of the German troops makes everything seem blighted and withered. People, too, are rather shabby, and, even when the shop windows are not boarded up there is next to nothing in them. Here and there some brave trades-people make a gesture, as the grocers, who show mainly shoe blacking and bug powder. Some jewellers show elaborate ornaments made of tin composition, and in the china shops you see bottles and plates made of wood. Via Condotti is desolate. No traffic goes down it except German cars and lorries; there are no chattering crowds near the shops, and no atmosphere of pleasant interest in life. The flower sellers on the Trinità steps make an effort to keep going, but it is daily harder, as there are no means of getting flowers by rail. Then too, prices are soaring. It is the same story as in Germany: there is too much paper money combined with a shortage of all goods, particularly food. The lira is worth next to nothing, six hundred being offered for a pound note, and 2,000 for a gold sovereign.

The presence of Allied prisoners, escaped from their camps after the armistice, is worrying the authorities considerably. Being active and resourceful they scattered in every direction, and have done remarkably well, considering their difficulties. Some have returned to the Allied lines, some are hidden in the hills and some in the towns. Everywhere they are treated like brothers. The peasants feed them, hide them, accompany them on their way, accepting no payment and often at the risk of great personal danger. One hopes that after the peace these peasants will get the recognition they deserve. There are plenty of ex-prisoners in Rome, and they are most efficiently taken care of. The civvies they wear are fearful and wonderful. I met one in Italian reach-me-downs with a fawn plush overcoat. He looked

[40]

much thinner than one would have wished. In spite of his fancy dress he had Sandhurst written all over him. He was going about Rome quite calmly.

An agitated official column in the press today reminds everyone that those who harbour Allied prisoners will be shot.

Friday October 22nd

A report which one can hardly believe says that the regular German troops are going and that we shall be left to the tender mercies of the S.S.

If you haven't got brains then hire some. The German failure to secure people for the labour service has not daunted them. They've had an idea. In the *Messaggero* a small advertisement has appeared in the "Situations Vacant" column: "German civil authorities want a specialist for propaganda and publicity, one familiar with the psychology of the workingman and who understands trade-union conditions. Apply Room 106, Albergo Ambasciatori from 9 to 12. Highest references required."

Saturday October 23rd

Another brave attempt was made today to get hold of Italian officers. On October 25th at the latest they must report at headquarters. After that date they will be court-martialled—provided they can be caught. "After that date," continues the proclamation, "a court-martial will deal with all those persons who hide them, feed them or give them any help whatsoever. All pensions hitherto paid to members of their families will be discontinued immediately." No stone is left unturned in this process of trying to discover where they all are. Plenty of people know, but won't tell.

Sunday October 24th

A perfectly new form of sabotage has been invented by the Roman patriots. It is decidedly inconvenient and puts everyone in a bad temper. Small change has disappeared from circulation, and rumours have been set afloat that the 1000-lire and 500-lire notes are counterfeit and will not be honoured by the Bank of Italy, so it is impossible to get them changed. And here the black market geniuses turn their usual dishonest penny: they offer you 900 lire in exchange for your 1000-lire note and 450 lire in exchange for a 500-lire note. The Republican "Government" is making a great fuss about it all, and is exhorting the Romans to pay no attention to reports, etc., etc. . . . They arrested the manager of the local telephone company, because he was found to have 133,000 lire in small change, and had ordered his personnel not to use it. The arrest was made by Guglielmo Pollastrini, himself one of the outstanding Fascist gangsters belonging to the Palazzo Braschi group.

Monday October 25th

And there was evening and morning one day.—Gen. I,5.

Tuesday October 26th

As we are past the 25th, date fixed as the last possible one on which Italian officers might report at headquarters, they are now allowed an extension of time until the 31st. If tragi-comedy has never been enacted in Rome before, it is taking place now.

A comprehensive programme of punishments to be meted out to civilians is published today. Here it is, in brief:

For harbouring or helping escaped prisoners of war: death.
For making contacts with them: hard labour for life.
For printing or publishing or circulating news derogatory to the prestige of the Axis Forces: penal servitude for life.
For owning a wireless transmitter: death.
For instructing wireless operators: hard labour for life.
For looting in evacuated areas: death.
For desertion of work, or sabotage: death.
For not fulfilling labour obligations: death.
For not acquainting the authorities of change of address: twenty years' prison.
For taking photographs out of doors: hard labour for life.

"The above sentences," continues the statement, "will be passed by court-martial." So now we know.

A good many of the S.S. have left. It seems that they are wanted in Berlin, where civil troubles may break out.

Some Italian patriots attacked German soldiers; ten of them were shot in reprisal.

Kesselring has been recalled to headquarters to report, and Stahel is to be replaced as commander of Rome by General Melzer. Stahel was, on the whole, a very decent man who tried to do all he could to keep his men under discipline in Rome, and disobeyed a number of Hitler's orders for "frightfulness." He was said to be a Catholic, but he is really an "Old Catholic," a sect founded by Döllinger in the 19th century. He was extremely respectful to the Pope. The newcomer may be worse.

The wireless from London tells us of some Allied progress in the South: Campobasso certainly was a valuable conquest. And we are moving forward along the Adriatic coast too. When will they get to Rome? We can only go on answering our Italian friends' desperate questionings with the confident assertion: "They know what they are doing." It will be awful if the Germans confiscate our wireless sets. They are the one link we have with the outside world, the one true source of information. People in the hotels have had to give their radios to the manager, who has them locked up under seals. Here we have one which could not be hidden, as it is registered, but we have a smaller one which could be concealed if a search were made; it isn't as powerful as the other, but it would be better than nothing. I suppose those broadcasters know what their news bulletins mean to us. One would like to say "thank you"; after the war is over we shall.

Thursday October 28th

The Germans have confiscated a Vatican truck with a trailer, and both sides are upset about it. It was bound for Pescara, full of empties, to collect flour and spaghetti, as the Vatican City has a right to provision itself independently of Rome. The truck had the Vatican license plate and flew the Vatican colours, but it was simply held up, the driver ordered to leave it and make his way home as best he could. The German Ambassador was sent for by the Secretary of State, Cardinal Maglione, who made a strong protest. The Ambassador made profound apologies, and there the matter rested. The truck was never traced, as von Weiszacker has no grip on the military. However, it probably will not happen again, as it seems that the Germans are anxious to propitiate the Vatican as much as possible; it looks as if they realized that when their collapse comes the Pope's would be the only voice which could be raised in their favour—always supposing he were willing to do so.

Friday October 29th

The difficulty of hiding patriots and Jews is becoming more and more acute. Time goes in seeing people who come streaming in for advice or introductions. It is physically impossible to hide anyone in this house of ours, but one can help in other ways.

We might have expected it. The S.S. men tried to search the Oriental Institute, the great centre for study of questions concerning the Eastern Churches, run by the Jesuits. The Rector speaks German fluently and forcefully; he met the S.S. group squarely.

"We have come for the Jewish workman in your employ," said the leader.

"He isn't here; he left us months ago."

"That's all right, we know all that of course, and we're going to search your premises just the same," was the rough answer.

"You're not going to search my premises. Are you aware that you are attempting to violate diplomatic immunity, and that this is extraterritorial property of the Holy See?"

At this the officer wilted ever so slightly, and muttered that he did not know it was pontifical property.

"By the way," continued the Rector, "are you under General Stahel's orders?" At this he looked a little more embarrassed and said:

"Er—no, we have our own special command," and withdrew, defeated.

It shows, strangely enough, that the S.S. have some respect for pontifical extraterritoriality, for all that they are Himmler's private army.

[44]

There is no salt and there are no matches. Such odd things to be suddenly lacking. Both salt and sulphur come from Sicily, so there you are. They are going to be rationed—whatever we shall get by that means. For it is one thing to have a ration card, and quite another to find the article in the shop where you are entitled to it. Sometimes the "rations" for one month are several months in arrears, and occasionally they skip out a month altogether. Lack of matches is hard for those who cook on gas (and most people do at present), because the gas goes on only for a brief period three times a day, and that means lighting up three times. There is talk of the ration being ninety matches a month —generally one third of them don't light. Smokers, who are to be allowed three cigarettes a day, will be allowed a few more matches. But of course the black market here comes into its own. Salt is to be had at 150 lire a kilo—its original price being 1 lira a kilo. Matches and cigarettes are any price you like to name.

Saturday October 30th

A tempting offer is made now by the men of the hills, peasants from the Abruzzi, who know the Apennines and are familiar with all sorts of mountain by-ways. For 8,000 lire they undertake to accompany you to the British lines in Southern Italy, seeing to everything on the way, food, lodging and travel. Of course you may have to do a good deal of the trip on foot so as to dodge the Germans, but, like any serious tourist agency, they promise to get you there safe and sound for the price. Sometimes they will take you to Terracina by land and then secure a fishing smack as far as Naples. A little while ago there was a regular service between Terracina and the Neapolitan and Sicilian ports, and on the Adriatic side there was one between places like Chioggia and Pescara to Bari; unfortunately the Germans discovered it, and their planes are on the lookout to machine-gun the ferry service; so at present it is much more risky than it used to be. If you are not inclined for travel, then they will take a letter for you to Naples and guarantee to bring back the answer for 500 lire—really a reasonable charge. In order to encourage mutual trust, with no nonsense about payment, when you give the peasant the letter you cut a 500-lire note in two, give him

[45]

one half and keep the other. When he returns with the answer you stick both halves together and hand them to him. So everyone is satisfied.

Sunday October 31st

R., who is attached to the Swiss Legation here, returning from Spain, has just brought us a parcel from a friend in Madrid. He said he had three more little parcels for us, but that they were in his luggage, which had been stopped at the frontier by the Germans. They don't mind who or what they stop at present. Considering that the parcels for us contain tea, I doubt if we ever see them. Oh, well—"*pazienza*," as they say locally.

Monday November 1st

The German authorities are being very, very kind to the Romans and have fixed the curfew from midnight until 5 A.M.; it was at 11 P.M., and has been as early as 9 P.M. The curfew, of course, has nothing to do with the blackout, in spite of the original meaning of the word; it simply indicates that everyone must be indoors. If you are out during it without a special permit you are either shot or arrested, probably the former. The blackout varies with the length of the days. Not that the blackout seems to matter as much as it used to; they are not anything like so particular about it as in the times when if the smallest gleam of light showed through a window, voices would be heard shouting "*Luce! Luce!*" until it was extinguished.

Tuesday November 2nd

As it is All Souls' Day the public is admitted to the Campo Verano, the great cemetery next to St. Lawrence-Outside-the-Walls, where so much damage was done in the first bombing of Rome on July 19th. No one had been allowed in since then, except two members of each family, because so many of the graves had been ripped open. It was one of the best cared-for cemeteries in the world, with superb flowers and plants of all kinds, kept up by the city authorities. They say that it will take ten years to get it back to its original condition. For today they erected barriers round the most damaged portions, and it all looked very desolate.

The Hotel Regina in Via Veneto has been requisitioned for the use of the Germans. It was quite full, and one can't imagine where all the guests have gone. The order was drastic and admitted of no delay.

Wednesday November 3rd

The 5th Army has not taken Isernia yet. They do seem very slow. Perhaps Isernia will really be a turning point, as they say, and we shall advance rapidly afterward. Things must move soon, surely.

Benedetto Croce, the hoary philosopher, is making himself heard loudly in demanding the abdication of the King. This isn't the moment for political shifts of that kind, and, after all, Italy will never succeed in being one republic. Only a monarchy can unite its divers provinces, in spite of all the philosophers and politicians.

Thursday November 4th

This morning a column of Germans passed down the Corso and went northward by the Via Flaminia; they held up the traffic for two hours. People stood looking at them in a dazed way, not daring to show their real feelings as the tanks and guns went by. Their columns are led by an officer in a small touring car who stands, holding up a red disc to show the way. The German radio made what some people consider to be a significant remark today. Speaking of air war in Italy, the broadcaster said: "If, in the heat of combat, bombs should fall on the Vatican City, we should be accused of wishing to murder the Pope, whereas in reality we would be defending Rome." It certainly provides matter for thought.

Friday November 5th

The Allied air force got that German column that left Rome yesterday. It was bound for Civitavecchia, and there was not much left when we had finished with it.

More hotels are being requisitioned by the Germans; they are of course taking them among the best and most comfortable, such as the Flora, the Excelsior, the Savoia and the Ambasciatori. Sometimes they take the whole building, sometimes a part of it. There are German sentinels at the doors. They have their court-martial as well as various offices at the Flora.

A tremendous propaganda effort is now being made regarding the art treasures and the archives of Monte Cassino. The Germans claim that they have put them in a secret place of safety, and that by so doing they are the saviours of civilization, etc., etc. Some say Spoleto is the place. They brought most of the monks by car and lorry to Rome, where they are lodged at the International College of Sant' Anselmo on the Aventine, and at the Abbey of St. Paul's-Outside-the-Walls. The Abbot and six monks have remained at Monte Cassino.

Saturday November 6th

They've done it. The Vatican has been bombed. Yesterday evening at about ten minutes past eight a plane flew low over the Vatican City and dropped four bombs in a more or less diagonal line running southeast to northwest. The damage is said to be extensive, but one can judge best at first hand; I hope to go there myself on Monday. The papers, naturally, publish columns of hysterical condemnation of the brutality of the British in daring to attack the Pope's own property and to endanger his life, not to speak of endangering the art treasures and the Basilica of St. Peter's. But in spite of all the printer's ink, and all the radio propaganda, the people of Rome are already saying with conviction *"i Tedeschi."*

Soon after it happened several important German officers presented themselves at the Vatican, full of concern, and ready to conduct a thorough investigation on the spot. Although the press stated that they did so, it was untrue, for their services were politely declined and they were not admitted. The strongest probability as to the identity of the pilot is that he was Farinacci's secretary flying a German plane. Farinacci is the old Fascist enemy of the Church, leader of the anti-clericals, and, at the present moment, uncrowned King of Cremona and Northern

Italy. He is acting as Mussolini's representative to the German authorities, and they do not mind what he does, provided he leaves their military arrangements undisturbed. Everybody knows that the Germans have numbers of English bombs in reserve for cases exactly like this. It seems fairly clear that they wanted to get the radio station, the only means by which the Pope can communicate freely with the outside world. But they missed it so completely that even the instruments were not damaged.

This morning, from half past ten onward, large groups collected in Piazza San Pietro beneath the windows of the Pope's study, cheering and shouting *"Evviva il Papa!"* and *"Il Papa! Il Papa!"* until at last he appeared at his window and gave them his blessing. He did so again at eleven and at half past eleven, as the crowd increased in numbers and in enthusiasm.

In the meantime, Cardinal Canali, President of the Pontifical Commission for the Vatican City; Prince Pacelli, Councillor, and Commendatore Galeazzi, Director of the Technical Department, made a thorough examination of the damaged premises.

Sunday November 7th

This morning all the parishes of Rome sent large groups of parishioners, each one headed by the parish priest himself, to Piazzo San Pietro, as a demonstration of sympathy and affection to the Pope. It was a dull rainy morning, but the crowd paid no attention to the weather. The Pope, at his accustomed work in his study, heard the cheers from the Piazza and told his secretary to look out of the window and report. On hearing what numbers of people were below he had his study window opened, the one which is directly behind his writing table, fifth from the end on the third floor of the great block of the Vatican Palace. When he was seen, all the umbrellas closed as if by magic and all the faces were raised toward him with a roar of cheering. As he held up his hand in blessing, a sudden silence fell and the words: "Benedicat vos omnipotens Deus Pater et Filius et Spiritus Sanctus" were distinctly audible. Then the cheering broke out again. As yesterday, so today he came back to the window twice at intervals of half an hour.

St. Peter's was open this morning. It had been closed on Saturday so that all the broken glass might be swept up, for the windows had suffered a good deal from the blast. There was no structural damage whatever to the dome or to the walls, contrary to a current report. Most glass was broken in the apse and the left transept. The great golden window with the dove, symbolic of the Holy Ghost, which occupies the centre of Bernini's "glory" in the apse, and which is the only stained glass in the entire church, was pierced by about twenty splinters, themselves of glass, blown in from its own large protecting window in the outer wall. The windows in the drum of the cupola whose heavy metal frames were strengthened quite recently, were fortunately slightly open for ventilation and were not harmed. On the other hand, some of the windows of the lantern of the cupola were blown in, although they are at a height of 120 metres.

The walls and dome may be safe, but one other thing has suffered severely in St. Peter's, and that is its climate. For the first time in history it was desperately cold inside the Basilica. The building is so vast and the ventilation managed with so much skill that it was always pleasantly cool in summer and warm in winter in comparison with the air outside. It will take some time to recover that Petrine climate, I fear. It was quite a shock to feel the cold on entering, not so much physically as psychologically. People crowded in this morning to hear the Masses which were being said as usual at the various altars.

Monday November 8th

The damage in the Vatican City was well worth investigating for oneself. Considering what it might have been, it was slight; considering the havoc wrought, it is not slight at all. One million lire worth of glass has been smashed, not to mention damage to dwellings; the destruction in the mosaic studio will take months and months to remedy.

Two of the Palatine Guard on duty on Friday evening saw the plane circle low over the Vatican City several times. It was flying at about 100 metres when it dropped the bombs. Although no public statement has been made everyone is convinced that it was a German plane; it was too dark at the time to recognize any markings it might have borne. It did not drop either incendiary or penetration bombs, but fragmentation bombs. The first one fell about thirty metres away from the building where Cardinal Canali lives, and fairly close to the city wall. All the Cardinal's windows were broken, naturally; his doors and shutters were blown in, and much damage was done to the interior by splinters. The windows in the courtyard of the neighbouring Palazzo Sta. Marta were broken, and, in the Palazzo dei Tribunali, just across the road, a big fragment of a bomb fell in the flat occupied by the Brazilian Ambassador. Numbers of diplomats took up residence in this building as the war became more widespread; they are those from China, Cuba, Peru, Bolivia, Venezuela, Uruguay and Ecuador.

The second bomb made a direct hit on the roof of the mosaic studio, which is half way between the apse of St. Peter's and the Vatican railway station. The damage here was very serious. The costly steel filing cabinet which was forged in Strasbourg and contains thousands of compartments for mosaic cubes of all shades was hit and the cubes were scattered; several unfinished pieces of work were destroyed; doors, windows and roof were smashed, and numbers of paintings damaged.

The most far-reaching explosion was that of the third bomb, which fell behind the Governor's Palace: besides windows, doors and shutters being destroyed, plaster fell from all the ceilings and inner walls and furniture were broken up. The retaining walls were, however, unshaken. The flat occupied by Mgr. Tardini, Secretary of the Congregation for Extraordinary Affairs, suffered severely, as did also the apartments reserved for visiting sovereigns.

The fourth bomb fell between the Ethiopian College and the radio station, and did no harm except to the reservoir. Windows were broken in the Vatican Museums, particularly in the Raphael Rooms and the sacristy of the Sistine Chapel. One Palatine Guard was wounded, otherwise there were no casualties.

Numbers of dignitaries called at the Vatican to express their sympathy; most of them were genuinely concerned, some were merely officious. Among the latter was the well known Gino Bardi, *Federale di Roma,* leader of the Roman Fascists, who came from his headquarters at Palazzo Braschi to offer his condolences.

Der Oberbefehlshaber General Feldmarschall Kesselring has issued an impressive list of "Orders for the Protection of the German Armed Forces," which runs as follows:

Information must be given at once to the German authorities (*Militaer-Platz, oder Ortskommandantur*—all in German) of:

a—The existence of or possession by anyone of arms, ammunition, or explosives of any kind.

b—Persons who are planning or who have executed acts of violence against members of the German armed forces, or against German organizations. Also of persons who have knowledge of the foregoing, together with their names and addresses.

c—The presence anywhere of members of enemy forces, and the names of those who harbour and assist them. The death penalty is established for those who do not give the foregoing information.

Moreover: for unlawfully wearing a German uniform or insulting or belittling the German armed forces the penalty is imprisonment.

Those who do not carry out or who neglect the supervision duties assigned to them by the Higher German Command will suffer the death penalty.

Thus one goes to prison for belittling a sensitive German soldier.

Wednesday November 10th

The telephones of all who reside in the streets nearest the Hotel Excelsior have been cut off, because of the German Command having quarters at the hotel. It looks as if they were afraid of spies.

The Vatican has sent a lorry north to get some glass to replace their million lire worth broken by the bombs the other day. In Rome glass is beginning to be on the black market.

Three more classes are called up for military service: those born in 1923, '24 and '25. They must report between the 15th and 30th of this month. That means that three more large groups of young men will go into hiding. Feeling against the Germans increases daily, and the idea of being forced to fight for them drives Italian men desperate. One does not count the infinitesimal but noisy neo-Fascist pro-German minority. They are out simply for what they can gain for the time being.

The British have broadcast today that they have now the complete report of the whereabouts of all Allied planes last Friday evening. None of them was near Rome.

Probably by way of illustrating German "protection" of the Vatican, last night the Vatican radio reported the fact that, since September, no mail has gone either in or out of Vatican City. It is an illuminating comment on the Germans' claim that they are facilitating everything for the Vatican authorities. And yet, they do clearly hope to propitiate the Pope as much as they can. There is no truth in the stories that they want him to leave Rome. Some individual Germans may have said so unofficially, but it is not the general view.

The Swiss press has stated that, on account of Friday's air attack, the families of the diplomats in the Vatican City had been directed to leave and were preparing to do so. The report is quite unfounded. No one is thinking of moving. The diplomats and their families are somewhat bored by the confinement and the limited resources of their place of residence, but would not think of leaving it.

The four reasons suggested by the British commentators for the bombing of the Vatican City by the Germans are unconvincing. They are: 1—To show the need for German "protection." 2—To show that it is unsafe for the Pope to remain there and thus have him removed elsewhere. 3—To give a pretext for taking away the art treasures of the Vatican, in order to put them in a safe place. 4—To induce the Pope to issue a protest against the bombing so worded as to cause misunderstanding between him and the Allies.

Thursday November 11th

The B.B.C. reports today that the whole quarter of Rome round Via Veneto has been mined by the Germans. If that is true, then this house, together with this diary, will soar skyward. We are definitely in the Via Veneto quarter.

From today onward there are no more taxis to be had on any pretext whatever. Those who still have bicycles are lucky.

Well, the Allies have crossed the Garigliano and have reached the German "winter line." Here the Germans are beginning to say: "We shall spend a happy Christmas in Rome and a happy Easter in Naples." *Vedremo:* we shall see.

Friday November 12th

Our enemy is determined to be comfortable here, anyway. Large truckloads of coal are being delivered at the hotels they have occupied; they seem to be very particular about heating. The rest of us can get no coal, and the weather is beginning to have a decided nip in it. In fact, by now, it is already a good deal colder indoors than out. These Roman houses with their marble or tiled floors, high ceilings and big windows are deadly cold when there is no means of heating them. The sun, when it is out, warms only the exact spot on which it shines.

Yesterday, in Via Regina Elena a crowd collected round a house from which came a desperate voice shouting: "Help! Help! I am an Italian officer!" There was no point in waiting until the shooting should begin, so one does not know the end of the poignant incident.

Saturday November 13th

Comic relief was provided by the London broadcast today. They said: "In Rome Italian patriots have occupied the catacombs and thence harry German troops." From the beginning everyone has known that the catacombs would be useless as hiding places; they could be smoked out like a badger's earth. It was thought at one time that the Germans would use gas if they considered it worth while to investigate the catacombs with it, but no one hid in them. And there is no harrying of German troops here. It would only lead to the bloodiest of reprisals, and would achieve nothing. The Roman patriots are wise enough to wait until there is immediate hope of the Allies occupying the city, and then they will come out in force, organized and armed. It is different in the North, where they are much more numerous and the Germans are less concentrated.

Sunday November 14th

Interesting information came in today about the escaped British prisoners in the hills outside Rome. There is a regular service which takes them parcels of clothes, books, food, medicines, etc., run by friendly Italian officers. Arrangements are made for their shelter, and the peasants build huts for them in the woods when it is too dangerous for them to stay in the villages. In some places each peasant going out for his day's work in the fields takes food for two people, enough for himself and enough for an Allied ex-prisoner. We know of an old peasant woman who always has one of them in her house, in honour of her son, who is a prisoner with the British. One enterprising man walked all the way from Verona to his own lines at Termoli. With the colder weather, however, which is coming on rapidly, they will have a good deal to suffer.

People arriving from Frascati tell us that they have not yet finished digging corpses out of the ruins after the air attack on September 8th.

Monday November 15th

The Germans have started arresting Poles in Rome. Possibly because the other day their President, speaking in London, referred to Polish friendship with all nations, and with "their great Eastern neighbour." Suspicion has, moreover, been brought on them by the espionage activities of a Polish lady and her two daughters. They were discovered, arrested and sent to the Mantellate, the prison for women, where they had a very hard time. Finally influence was brought to bear by some of their friends, and they were transferred to another place. One hopes that the other Poles will not be locked up on their account. It is a platitude to say "You never know what Germans will do."

Tuesday November 16th

Crossing Ponte Vittorio this afternoon we saw two superb rainbows over Castello Sant'Angelo against a sky of steely grey; symbolic perhaps of the good fortune that awaits both the 8th and the 5th armies.

[55]

War correspondence quoted by the B.B.C. says: "It will be a tough job to take Cassino, but when we have done so then we shall be truly on the road to Rome." Yes, certainly. But first catch your hare. The Germans know the value of Cassino. Our electrician remarks pessimistically: "They will try to hold the Allies down there until they have finished robbing us in these parts, and when there is nothing left here to steal, then they will withdraw." This appears to be the general opinion in his circle.

A few Jews have been allowed to return to their homes, largely on account of action taken by the Pope. Is it possible to hope that the man-hunting is over?

Wednesday November 17th

No, it isn't possible to hope for what I wrote yesterday. The Germans have caught three thousand men who were hiding in caves in the campagna near the Madonna del Devin'Amore at Castel di Leva. They intend to make round-ups whenever they can. These people were not Jews; the Germans wanted them for their "labour service."

Thursday November 18th

It now takes ten days for the news of the death of a Bishop in Umbria to reach the Vatican, in spite of what the Germans call perfect freedom of communication. This was the case with the death of Mgr. Estorre of Nocera Umbria who died at Sassoferrato.

Friday November 19th

Strange statements are made by the Swiss press. They have correspondents in Chiasso who apparently cannot verify Roman news. *La Liberté* of Fribourg reports that the Governor of the Vatican City has caused the following notice to be affixed to the three entrances:

The Governor of the Vatican City by order of Cardinal Luigi Maglione, Secretary of State, declares that this place is a way of access to the Vatican City, a sovereign, independent and neutral state. In consequence it enjoys the right of inviolability.

Under this notice, in Italian, continues *La Liberté*, is a German translation of it, and a declaration by General Stahel, the commander in Rome, forbidding members of the Wehrmacht to enter the City.

None of this is authentic. The three entrances have no notices but at each stand two Swiss Guards, one of whom carries a rifle. All who wish to enter have to give full proof of their identity and their business before a pass is issued. This pass is examined at frequent intervals by officials in uniform and in plain clothes, as the bearer goes on his way. The pass must be given up at the exit.

No German soldiers may cross the white line outside the colonnade which marks the Vatican City boundary. There are often groups of them assembled at that point, waiting to be shown round St. Peter's; they are taken there by priests who have special qualifications for the purpose. When the visit is over they are punctiliously escorted back to the boundary line by their ecclesiastical guide.

The mistake about the notice was probably made because all buildings in Rome which are "extraterritorial," that is, the property of the Holy See and therefore enjoying diplomatic immunity, bear a placard in Italian and in German: "Property of the Holy See. Extraterritorial zone," and they also have one of the Palatine Guards on duty at the entrance. Each religious house, other than extraterritorial, has been given a document signed by both the Vatican and the German authorities to the effect that, being such, it is not to be searched; but these documents are not displayed. The only building which bears a notice in German only, forbidding the *Wehrmacht* to enter, is the Quirinal Palace.

Saturday November 20th
It is pouring rain. The Sangro and the Garigliamo are in flood. We've had days and days of this, and it looks as if we would

have more. One can't blame the Americans in the 5th army, who say that the first thing they will do on reaching home is to go to the Italian tourist agencies and tear up all the posters that represent Italy as the Land of Eternal Spring. The Allies seem stuck in front of Cassino. Leros has surrendered. There is that unnecessary trouble with the French in the Lebanon. Everyone is horribly depressed. "The Allies won't be here before Easter, mark my words." "The Germans are planning to retake Naples." "Why can't we get a move on?"

A futile "Constituent Assembly" presided over by Il Duce was held in the North the other day, although many say that Mussolini is dead.

Yesterday Frau Kesselring was shown round the Vatican Museums by the Director, Professor Nogara. It was a great compliment to her, as the Museums are closed to the public at present.

The Austrian soldiers have been deprived of their revolvers and are left with their bayonets only. Numbers of them have deserted already and are wandering about in the hills. It appears that a large band of them, together with Allied ex-prisoners and Italian patriots, under the command of a former German officer, are in the hills near Spoleto conducting guerrilla warfare. It may quite well be the case, though one has no means of being certain of it.

Sunday November 21st

We have begun to take refugees into our house; it is simply impossible to refuse. These are Sicilians from near Syracuse, and, as they were bombed by the Allies, I suppose we ought to do something about it. The food question is the crux. We made a strong appeal to the Vatican for help in feeding them, and got a sack of flour and a sack of potatoes. The latter are almost a luxury.

Provisions are increasingly hard to get. Nearly everything is rationed, but no one could live on the quantities allotted in the rationing, and even then, the shops where one has registered under the rationing scheme often do not have the things one has a right to. At present we have had only half the *pasta* (macaroni or spaghetti) which was due in October. None of the November rations has been available yet, with the exception of bread (150 grammes a day) and a small amount of lard. Very little sugar is allowed, half a pound per month per person; and the tenth part of a litre of oil. Green vegetables are difficult, if not impossible, to find, and there is no question of fruit, fresh or canned. Flour and rice are to be had in the black market at terrific prices. Potatoes can be got in the same way, but rarely. Even the black market has hardly any jam; and milk, fresh, condensed or desiccated, is next to unobtainable. There is no meat or fish, fresh or preserved, nor eggs, except the latter on the black market. Tea, coffee and cocoa just aren't there, unless you are prepared to pay a couple of thousand lire a kilo.

However, we and our refugees manage to get along and to find enough for two meals a day (one hesitates to count breakfast as a real meal here and in these circumstances), even if they do lack some of the dishes we might be having in peace time. We have great hopes of the Allies helping with our commissariat when they arrive; we hear that in the south they have brought plenty of tinned things, which we shall welcome heartily. One seems to notice the absence of tea and coffee most of all. The substitutes used for coffee are pathetic; the best of them is barley roasted and ground. The colour is all right and it is wet, but that is about all that can really be said for it, unless it contains a little sustenance, as the experts claim. Imitation tea is made of camomile, lime leaves or blackberry leaves, or else dried orange peel, roasted and grated. Like the coffee, when you get it, it is hot and wet and very, very unconvincing, particularly when there is no milk nor sugar to go with it.

It stopped raining today, and optimists are foretelling a big action somewhere soon. *Magari:* would that it might be true.

Monday November 22nd

The Turkish Embassy is leaving Rome. This may mean that Turkey intends to enter the war, or it may be that they are following the "Government" to the north of Italy. There is a great fuss about the departure of the Ministries; and functionaries who prefer to await the coming of the Allies in Rome rather than follow the precarious fortunes of Mussolini's exalted yes-men have lost their jobs. Pressure even is brought to bear to induce them to travel, and much higher salaries are offered to those who will consent to go to Verona or Venice or Cremona, wherever the particular organization happens to have settled.

The Germans are still fiercely searching houses for hidden arms, motor cars and men.

Tuesday November 23rd

War, as has frequently been said before, involves all sorts of unexpected consequences. In Rome, the steady deterioration of buses and trams is one of them. There are no spare parts, rubber is lacking for tires, brake linings wear out and stay worn out, more vehicles are scrapped, more people try to get on the remaining ones, and the strain breaks them down sooner than usual. Yesterday evening there was a horrible accident to the tram that passes below the Pincio, beside the outward-sloping piece of the old city wall known as Muro Torto. Before reaching Piazza del Popolo there is a long slope and a curve, and the track passes close to a low brick wall that surrounds Villa Borghese. It was dark, and the heavily laden tram had gained such momentum that the brakes would not act. It reached the curve at full speed, swung off the tracks, crashed into the wall and collapsed on its side among the débris. The wounded passengers lay there helpless until another tram came along.

The Germans are making "scorched earth" of Fregene, cutting down the pines and destroying the olives. It is one of the most charming seaside places within easy reach of Rome, with famous pine woods near the beach.

Wednesday November 24th

Yesterday we heard very heavy explosions in the distance, and we learned today that it was the Allies bombing out all that was left of the big airfield of Ciampino, about fourteen kilometres from here, on the way to Frascati. The planes that came over looked like dragon-flies in the sun. It is doubtful if it will be possible to use the airfield again, even after several months of repairing. The field itself, the hangars, the repair shops, the sheds for stores, everything was blown up. The anti-aircraft guns were very active, but not the Luftwaffe.

Thursday November 25th

Our spell of fair weather was deceptive. It is raining in torrents here, and they say it is worse in the South and on the Adriatic.

Mussolini and his Council of Ministers met again yesterday, somewhere in the North. The papers came out with big headlines about it, which is a consideration, when there is only one sheet to the whole paper. Their decisions were published in full. The name of the Italian State in future is to be "Italian Social Republic," and workers' salaries are to be raised by 30 per cent. They have, of course, no hope of stemming the tide of inflation as they had at the beginning of the war, so as prices rise they raise salaries, hoping for the best and prepared to stand from under when the crash comes. They have also established a special court to try the members of the Grand Council who voted against Mussolini on July 25th. It will go hard with the latter if they are caught. Some, it seems, have left the country.

Friday November 26th

Once more the Jews: all objects of art belonging to them are declared to be sequestered by the nation.

The Pope has received the British Minister, the American representative, and the German Ambassador. In consequence rumour says that Hitler is trying to negotiate peace. The probability is that these audiences are merely routine, or rather war-routine ones.

A humourous feature of the present situation is the avalanche of requests for English lessons. Today alone five sets of people have called to ask for information about where they can be had. Fortunately we have the addresses of several hard-working teachers who are delighted to get extra work. Some of the applicants say quite frankly: "We want to know how to welcome the Allies when they come."

Saturday November 27th

German truck and motor drivers are reckless beyond all description. They killed Renato Cialente, a very popular actor, yesterday evening, and the Romans are furious. He was coming away from the Teatro Argentina with some friends; they were walking quietly down the Corso, not in the road but on the pavement, when a German lorry dashing along swerved and knocked him down, fracturing his skull. Death was instantaneous. The city was shocked by his tragic death, and everyone loudly blamed the Germans for it. German trucks are the only ones allowed on the Corso, so there could be no question of the driver's nationality. One paper raised its voice with no uncertain sound, and although censorship is rigid here, its protests were printed. The *Voce d'Italia* said:

This unhappy death throws fresh light on the brutal irresponsibility of drivers who speed recklessly, even during the blackout, without the slightest regard for the safety of pedestrians. A recent military ordinance limited the speed of vehicles, particularly in the more central quarters; we do not know if the orders have been withdrawn, but apparently drivers of motors, and particularly of trucks, care nothing about them, judging from the increasing number of street accidents. We witness accidents of this type daily because careless drivers, *even military ones*, disregard pedestrians crossing the streets. Human lives seem no longer to be of any account, if the first motor driver who comes by, though he be wearing *a military uniform*, can thus butcher foot passengers. We beg for energetic action in this matter on the part of both civil and military authorities. [The italics are mine.]

Sunday November 28th

We are all encouraged by the message General Montgomery has sent to his men: "The time has come to drive the Germans north of Rome. They have been outfought, and we can now go forward." Certainly the time has come. In fact we feel it is a trifle overdue.

Monday November 29th

The High Command at the Hotel Excelsior is bright and cheerful. Officers of incredible elegance make their way in and out, sentries snap to the salute, and a good time is had by all. General Maelzer gave an entertainment on quite a large scale there yesterday evening, with the help of Italian actors and singers. It was organized by a producer from Berlin, distinguished for the management of the "Komiker Kabarett." Elaborate refreshments for all and plenty of flowers for the ladies were forthcoming.

They're losing men by the hundred in Italy and by the thousand in Russia, but the Komiker Kabarett must go on. One wonders if that sort of revelry by night is inseparable from war. Perhaps so.

Tuesday November 30th

The neo-Fascists are causing themselves to be despised and hated somewhat more than previously by what has just come out about the doings at their headquarters in Palazzo Braschi. Having got wind of something unusual going on there, the Germans, direct and forceful as usual, sent for some members of the Italian police, and together they raided the place. The resident Fascists were dumbfounded, so was the raiding party. In the cellars they discovered a number of non-Fascists, men of good standing and reputation, in a pitiable condition from imprisonment, starvation and torture. Some details of the torture are too revolting for description. Some of the prisoners had died and their bodies had been disposed of inside the building. Several, who could still move, jumped from the windows when the raid began, and were taken to the hospital with broken limbs. Besides their victims, the Fascists had also concealed quantities of gold, silver and jewels which they had "sequestered" by entering houses and demanding them at the point of the revolver. They also had, as might have been expected, large supplies of foodstuffs, flour, ham, cheese, wine, oil and other things which are severely rationed.

No mention was made in the press of the immediate arrest of the Palazzo Braschi gang, but in less than twenty-four hours the whole of Rome knew about it and feeling ran high. Forty in all were taken off to prison and shipped to the North for trial. The ringleaders were the famous "Federale dell'Urbe" Gino Bardi, who had hastened to present condolences to the Pope on behalf of the Roman Fascists when the Vatican was bombed; the two Pollastrini, father and son; Carlo Franquinet; Guido Strappafelci; Eros Conti; Mario Caruso; Cesare de Paolis and Sante Marchetti. The general comment was: "Well, anyway, the Germans have done one good deed in arresting those blackguards."

Wednesday December 1st

More posters today telling us what not to do. The prohibition was published long ago, but as the public paid no attention whatever, they have now put it on the walls. We are informed that we MUST NOT listen to broadcasts from countries that are not occupied by Germans. This is a new way of expressing it; they used to say "enemy countries." Moreover we MUST NOT spread anti-German news. They don't specify just what anti-German news is; anyway, we mustn't spread it. The penalty is a heavy fine and/or imprisonment.

It is coming out by degrees that the Germans are less and less enthusiastic about the Fascists, and that, if they possibly could, they would get rid of them altogether. Unfortunately Il Duce is Der Fuehrer's friend, so they can't. If it were not for that "friendship" Fascists would have disappeared some time ago, and the Germans would be governing occupied Italy in name as well as in deed.

Thursday December 2nd

The "Republic" has abolished all titles and honours conferred by the "ex-King of Italy," but graciously allows Pontifical titles and honours to be recognized and used, in the same way as foreign titles are recognized. In all probability there is going to be a slight hitch concerning this and various other things before long, as the Pontifical Government has not recognized the "Italian Social Republic" and the latter is sore about it.

Friday December 3rd

We cling to straws here. Everyone is excited and pleased because there is a persistent rumour of the Germans' withdrawal.

It originated in the fact that there are lots of Germans in the streets, and some of them are asking their way. Because they don't know Rome it was concluded that they were passing through on their way to the North. Also, they have forced the evacuation of Cassino, as if they were going to destroy it before leaving. The Cassinese people had no choice and no time. At the point of a gun they were told to leave or be shot, so they climbed into the German lorries and were taken off. Numbers of them arrived in Rome and were dumped in the suburb of Tor Pignattara, bewildered, cold, hungry and exhausted. No provision had been made for them, so they just stood there. Convents came to the rescue and the nuns took the refugees in, at least for the time being and until something definite could be arranged.

The nuns here have been magnificent in the midst of bombardments, evacuations and other tragic circumstances of war. With superhuman strength of mind and body, in the teeth of chaos they have organized, and in the teeth of famine they have fed the hungry and harboured the shelterless. Indeed mute and inglorious they have been and are. Individuality is hidden beneath the uniforms they wear; they are not out for medals or ribbons or recognition; but if people in the Allied countries salute women in uniform, they certainly ought to salute women wearing the religious dress, when they get here, at last. The salute will have been earned.

Today the Vatican daily, the *Osservatore Romano*, publishes a strong protest against the treatment of Jews; it is called forth by the new directions issued by the "Republic" to the heads of the Provinces, to the effect that all Jews must be sent to concentration camps. The order was issued obviously at the instigation of the Germans. The *Osservatore* points out that it is unreasonable, unchristian and inhuman. Times are bad enough, it says, without our creating fresh sources of suffering and anxiety; we are sorely in need of God's help, which we can gain by exercising charity toward His creatures, and all of us, nations as well as individuals, are in need of that today. Let us take care to be just and merciful, it concludes, and to pay our own debts so that God may remit ours with both justice and mercy.

It was a bold protest, courageously made. The *Osservatore* is sold regularly on all the Roman news-stands, and, strange to say, it continues to be sold, even after publishing articles as outspoken as this.

Saturday December 4th

The Roman German-controlled press answered the *Osservatore* by asserting that Jews were considered foreigners, and as such they were potential enemies and therefore might with perfect justice be sent to concentration camps. This evening's *Osservatore* replies firmly that no decree issued by any political party can change the status of an Italian-born citizen, possessing his nationality by the existing laws of the land; and that, even if enemy aliens were to be sent to concentration camps, the old and infirm, women and children, are exempt. The article is both judicious and moderate, and ends with the words: "We shall continue to place our trust in wisdom and good will, in justice and mercy; if these are carried into effect all will be spared fresh cause for anxiety, and the end will be equally well attained. From good deeds done, good will accrue to all."

Sunday December 5th

The *Osservatore* protests once more, this time on both sides. The editor deplores the murder, which took place yesterday, of Colonel Gino Gobbi in Florence; he was the Fascist commander of the city police. But, as "reprisals," ten anti-Fascists were executed immediately. Condemning this ferocious act of revenge, the writer says: "If this method is followed, then the numerical increase of reprisals and counter-reprisals will end in mass executions of men by the hundred or even by the thousand, and will lead to absolute disregard of human life as such."

Yesterday, for the first time, mention was made in the Roman press of the crimes committed at Palazzo Braschi. It was stated that the police had completed the arrest of "individuals guilty of grave indiscipline and of illegal activities, of disturbing public order and of bringing discredit on the local Fascist group."

Monday December 6th

Our baker's boy arrived this morning with his hand and arm bandaged. When asked what had happened he said laconically: "A German truck."

Roads in and out of Rome are carefully guarded by armed German sentries, and a list of roads which may be used is published. The larger ones are open day and night; smaller ones only in the daytime, and footpaths may not be used at all. They want to put a stop to cross-country escapes.

Tuesday December 7th

There is nothing really amusing about being robbed, thought the Trappists, whose monastery lies between Rome and Albano, when the Huns swept off their livestock consisting of a horse, a cow and a pig. Being vowed to perpetual silence, they just said nothing and carried on as best they could without the animals. Twenty-four hours after the theft, in the dawn's early light, they saw a strange procession returning to their house: the horse, followed by the cow, followed by the pig, all alone, and, like their masters, in silence. The Germans are still wondering wistfully what happened to them, being particularly partial to fresh pork.

Wednesday December 8th

The news man whose stall is opposite our house is poorer than most, having a family of five to support on what he makes or doesn't make. This morning when he opened up, he found several children in a basket awaiting his arrival, while two adults stood guard over them. It turned out that they were relatives of his from Cassino, evacuated by the Germans, and like those dropped in the road at Torpignattara, stood waiting until some help should be forthcoming. They had no food, no shelter, no ration cards, and very few clothes. The news man simply took them into his own overcrowded lodging. We managed to help out with bedding, food and money. On occasions like this the charity of the poorest to one another is an example to us all.

Rumours grow with the speed and facility of mushrooms. The latest one is that the German Command has had no news from Hitler for four or five days, and that, if his silence continues for two days more, they will take it upon themselves to withdraw from their positions here. They have concluded, so says the rumour, that Hitler was either caught in the air attack on Berlin or has fled.

Friday December 10th

Strangely enough the Germans have made good their boast about saving the treasures of the Abbey of Montecassino. It is difficult to understand their motives, after their wanton destruction of the great library at Naples. Anyway, here are the treasures in countless cases and boxes: archives, manuscripts, books, pictures, engravings and illuminated missals. There are about a hundred thousand volumes in all, not counting the manuscripts. The sight was striking and picturesque when the long line of heavily laden lorries came down the Tiber embankment and passed beneath the battlemented walls of Castel Sant'Angelo and through the gate into the court of the old fortress. German officials made a speech or two, somebody answered them on behalf of the "Ministry of National Education," and the transfer was accomplished. These precious things will all be housed in the Vatican Library as soon as it is convenient. It is providential that, at the present moment, the Vatican Library should be closed to readers. The members of the staff are thus free to deal with these incoming books and manuscripts. Moreover, an increasing number of Roman princes are giving their family archives to the Pope for the Vatican Library, and this makes still more work for the staff. The donors follow the example of Don Gelasio Caetani who, shortly before his death, presented the vast Caetani archives to Pope Pius XI; they now occupy one entire room in the Library. It is felt that all these archives will be in safe keeping, that they will be classified, catalogued and made available for research. No other Library can compare with the Vatican Library, and if anything should happen to it in this war the loss to civilization would be inexpressible. A movement is on foot at present to reproduce all their existing manuscripts on microfilm as a precaution against possible destruction.

Saturday December 11th

There is a new German way of dealing with men who dodge the labour service. They will get no ration cards. These cards are issued every four months; probably a census will be taken before they are due next time, and all who are not working will have to starve quietly. On the other hand, so little is available at times of what is apportioned by the cards that some say frankly: "Keep your card, we don't want it—for all that we get to eat by means of it we might as well be without," and they are untouched by the new penalty.

Sunday December 12th

The city authorities hope to remedy the food shortage, or so they say, not only by obliging all producers to sell their products to the general store of food, at the established prices of course, but also by forbidding provisions to be brought into Rome without a special permit. The sentries on the roads leading to the city will be responsible for carrying out the new regulation. Individuals may bring in three kilogrammes of food for personal consumption. This legislation constitutes a well meant effort to stop black market transactions. Of course it will have no effect on the black market except to send up the prices.

Monday December 13th

Today we are faced with another attempted remedy for another increasing difficulty. The remedy is comparable only to King Canute's gesture ordering the waves to recede. So as to relieve the violently congested condition of the buses, it is arranged now for the bus stops to be five hundred metres farther apart than formerly. The authorities point out hopefully that this will make people willing to walk all the way, as they would have to go so far to get the bus. The answer is simply that they won't, and the buses will be as bad as ever—or probably worse.

Tuesday December 14th

The German Ambassador to the "Republic" has presented his credentials personally to Il Duce somewhere in the North. He is the truculent Dr. Randolph von Rahn, a specialist in "occupations" accompanied by drastic measures. He was very active when Paris was occupied, and was Chargé d'Affaires here before the armistice, when the Ambassador was absent.

We found it necessary to dig up one of our boxes of buried valuables today. It contained money and securities. Setting out light-heartedly, we dug. No box. We dug farther around the spot. No box. Feverishly we tried to remember if any thief could possibly have seen us at the job when we buried the box. Had the gardener discovered it accidentally and made off with it? We dug on. The ground was rooted up as if by a maddened terrier. No box. Darkness fell, and we gave it up for the time being.

Wednesday December 15th

After a sleepless night we went on digging. No box. We gave ourselves up to the resignation of despair, but made one more try, deeper and yet farther from the spot. The box!—And the moral of that is, when you bury valuables in time of war, mark the spot carefully.

Food transport is becoming so difficult that the old method of using the Tiber for the purpose is being advocated on all sides. If only they could organize it properly, the thing would work admirably. Barges loaded with produce from Umbria could be brought down with the current and return upstream empty. There will be a real famine here soon if they don't do something of the sort.

Thursday December 16th

The Roman Fascists have moved their headquarters to the fine building in Via Veneto which used to be the seat of the Ministry of Corporations. They have thus shaken the dust of Palazzo Braschi, of evil memory, from their feet forever, and to white-wash it as far as possible, it is to be turned over to evacuees from southern Italy. These are the personal directions given by the new Federale, Giuseppe Pizzirani, who succeeded Gino Bardi, the leading gangster, now under arrest.

We were talking today of the slow progress of the Allies both on the 5th and the 8th army fronts, and someone pointed out that in over two thousand years of its history Italy had never been invaded from the south, except by Belisarius in the sixth century when he overthrew the Gothic kingdom. It is the slowest and most difficult way of conquering the country. And, moreover, the Germans are defending their positions with grim determination, apparently in order to have something to compensate for their débâcle in Russia.

Friday December 17th

The Montecassino treasures are being moved from Castel Sant' Angelo to the Vatican. We saw some of them going this morning as we crossed Ponte Vittorio.

There are so many German cars of every description and so many German soldiers going about the streets that it looks as if the soldiers marched round and round for propaganda purposes, and the drivers of cars were told to show themselves as much as possible. Via Sistina is the headquarters of their Transport Command, and it is alive with them. Among us it is known as Brighter Berlin. Piazza della Trinità, at the upper end, is blocked with their conveyances, from smart stolen cars for the officers to trucks for the men. The printed notices there are all in German, and there is a German military traffic policeman at the lower end, where Via Sistina runs into Via Francesco Crispi.

Saturday December 18th

Minor repairs to the Vatican radio apparatus on account of some slight damage caused during the air raid of November 5th have now been completed. The experts in charge there have decided to set up an emergency station in case of more attacks of the same kind. Thus there should always be the possibility of communicating with other countries by means of one station or the other.

We have just learned that on Thursday night there was a big

explosion in the Fascist barracks in Viale Romania, near Piazza Ungheria. It was presumably a time bomb, but the Fascists don't seem to be able to trace the man who put it there. They always say "communists" when these things happen.

This morning another bomb went off in a little eating house in Piazza Risorgimento, where some Germans were having dinner; they were all killed. Two Fascists were murdered yesterday; one of them was shot, as he was walking along the street, by a cyclist who came up from behind, fired, and was off at full speed.

This evening, more explosions. At about six o'clock, a time bomb which had been placed in the elevator shaft of the Hotel Flora went off, killing one German soldier, and one woman, and injuring several others. The Flora is being used as headquarters by the Germans at present, and Kesselring lodges there when he is in Rome. He was there today and escaped as if by miracle, as he escaped during the bombing of Frascati; he seems to have a charmed life.

Considerable injury was done to the hotel by the explosion, particularly to the heating plant. Hot water oozed from the walls and poured from damaged pipes, in all directions. The Germans were very particular about having their rooms well warmed in this chilly weather, and they wanted hot water. Well, they got it.

There was tremendous excitement in Via Veneto when it all happened. Every passer-by, whether on foot or in a motor, was arrested and hustled into one of the ground-floor rooms of the hotel. No one was allowed to telephone home to say why they were detained, and they were not told how long they might be kept there. All were interrogated minutely, and those who were considered suspicious were kept all night. One of our friends who was there got away at 8.15, because she could talk German. The Spanish Ambassadress to the Holy See, who was passing in her motor at the time, was stopped and brought into the hotel like everybody else. It was some minutes before she was allowed to go. Voluble apologies followed, and it was explained that she had been led into the hotel for safety. But that was a lie.

This morning another time bomb went off in the cinema in Piazza Barberini and killed a civilian; it naturally caused a panic as well.

Today's papers publish orders from the German Command of Rome that the curfew, instead of beginning at 11.30 P.M. and ending at 5 A.M., will now begin at 7 P.M. and end at 6 A.M. This is the city's punishment for bomb-throwing. We are "confined to barracks" after 7 o'clock. That means that the trams will start their last trips at 5.30. It dislocates everything, especially for the unfortunates who do not eat in their own houses; their evenings will be hungry ones indeed.

There are barricades and sentinels in front of the Flora and the Excelsior hotels, and the former is provided with machine guns as well. No one may pass on the pavement in front of them. Residents in the upper part of Via Veneto, that is between Via Ludovisi and Porta Pinciana, are punished worse than most, because for them the curfew begins at 5 P.M.

The work-people explain these murders by saying: "Well, what can you expect? The Germans are starving us."

Monday December 20th

The press passionately urges all citizens, in the name of *"risponsabilità e civismo"* to treat the Germans nicely and not to attack them. We hear hand grenades and rifle shots at night around the new Fascist headquarters close by in Via Veneto, but they are mysterious shots and we never hear either the exact cause or the results. Of course it is a strain on the Romans, wrought up as they are against the Germans and possessed by political passion, not to shoot when a good occasion offers. They do not stop to consider that, apart from other things, they will bring down on their fellow-citizens far heavier penalties than their action would warrant, and that they are doing nothing thereby to win the war.

The German Command today forbids the use of bicycles between 5 P.M. and 7 A.M. This is a blow for the working men who used to cycle to and from their work, that is, those whose machines had not been stolen by the Germans. Of course those cyclist murders brought this on everybody.

It is announced that the Pope will broadcast on Christmas Eve. What can he say? Everyone wonders. And it is also announced that the Midnight Masses which used to be celebrated on Christmas Eve will be anticipated and said at five o'clock in the afternoon.

Wednesday December 22nd

Unpleasant news this morning. The patriots and Jews who have been sheltered in religious houses all over Rome will probably not be safe any more. The Fascists—not the Germans this time—are raiding them. Back in October, when the S.S. men first got here, they tried to search the Oriental Institute, but desisted on learning it was pontifical property. The "Republican Fascists," on the other hand, are quite free from such scruples, and enjoy breaking into anything belonging to the Pope because they are so very, very sensitive at not having had their "Government" recognized by the Vatican. As far as the Vatican is concerned, politically the "Republicans" simply aren't there, and it, as it were, just looks over their heads when they come up to shake hands. They are terribly upset about it, now adopting the attitude: why-should-*we*-recognize-the-Vatican-anyway?—coolly brushing aside the Lateran Treaty, signed by Mussolini in 1929.

This, their first venture, was on a fairly large scale, including three neighbouring establishments. The Lombard College, founded by Pope Pius XI for Church students from his own Province, the Oriental Institute run by the Jesuits, and the Russicum, the College for Russian Church students, form one large block of pontifical property close to St. Mary Major's.

There was a spy among the patriots at the Lombard College who arranged everything for the entrance of the Fascists. A number of the patriots were arrested, though several got away by the back stairs. The house was thoroughly searched, and the leader of the gang confronted the Rector with a revolver and a letter from a girl to whom one of the refugees was engaged.

"These are nice things to be found in the table drawers of your so-called church students," he sneered.

Some of the patriots are unquestionably imprudent, as in the case just mentioned. We heard of another incident in which an Italian officer, hiding from the Germans, was taken in by some friends of ours at their own great risk. Toward evening his wife rang him up to know how he was. Every telephone in the city is supervised. One may imagine the result of such indiscretions.

At the Oriental Institute, the Jesuits had sheltered three Jews. The Brother porter faced the Fascists and said: "You have no right here, this is pontifical property. Where are your papers?"

"Here," was the answer, and the Brother found himself looking into the muzzle of a revolver. During the search one of the Jews escaped. The second was suffering from heart disease, and collapsed from shock of being discovered. The third was a doctor, and although he could have escaped quite easily he would not leave the man who had fainted. They were both taken.

Only three were caught in the Russicum, but it was searched like the other two houses. As he was going, the leader of the gang turned to the Rector and said: "Why did you hide these men?"

"For the same reason for which we shall probably be hiding you before long," said the Rector.

As the "Fascist Republic" has no representative at the Vatican, the only way in which the latter can protest against this flagrant violation of diplomatic immunity is through the German Ambassador. As a matter of fact, the Germans are thoroughly sick of the Fascists, and if it were not for the personal friendship—whatever it may amount to—between Hitler and Mussolini, they would have got rid of them long ago and ruled without them. Just when the Germans are doing their best to conciliate the Vatican, the Fascists go and upset everything. There is no doubt whatever about this desire on the part of the Germans.

Thursday December 23rd

The "Midnight" Masses which were to be said at 5 P.M. tomorrow have been cancelled in all the parishes, on account of the curfew and in order not to have crowds collecting in the afternoon.

Most of the patriots on the run in Rome hardly ever spend

more than a night or two now in the same place. Their wives and children also go to live away from home, because otherwise they might be taken as hostages. The porters tell enquiring Fascist and Gestapo agents that they have gone and they have no idea where they are. The way they escape arrest is wonderful, under the circumstances. Naturally they all have false papers. The police had the happy thought of taking the list of addresses of friends hanging near the telephones when they searched the houses, but even those were destroyed by the prudent ones.

Some of the police force are patriots at heart and do a good deal to help the others. One of them began his conversation with an anti-Fascist's wife by saying significantly: "Your husband is *not* here, is he?" "No," said she. "Then that is all," he answered, "I have done my duty," and went.

An order, published today, is intended to prevent this perpetual flitting of patriots or Jews. Here it is:

1—All changes of domicile in the city of Rome are forbidden, without special authorization of the police.
2—House owners or their responsible agents must make a full list of all persons resident in each house, floor by floor, and place it in a conspicuous position in the entrance.
3—Anyone giving hospitality to persons other than those included in the above-mentioned lists will be punished according to German military law.

The census of the population of Rome is to be taken at once.

Friday December 24th

At ten o'clock this morning the Pope received the Cardinals of the Curia, who presented their Christmas wishes to him. As a rule, in his answering speech he mentions any matters of importance which he wishes to make known. Today he made a brief review of the damage done to Rome and to the Vatican City from the air, and urged his hearers to use all their influence in order that the citizens might keep calm and self-controlled in whatever trials might await them in the future.

At a quarter past twelve the Pope made his broadcast to the world. Seated at the table in his private study, he spoke clearly and distinctly. The Italian stations relayed his speech, so that everyone heard it, both inside and outside Italy. The speech was dignified and penetrating, on the evils of war and the need for peace on the sound basis of Christian principles, and it carried conviction in unexpected quarters. But will the conviction be acted upon?

The Germans, out of the kindness of their hearts, are giving the Romans a Christmas treat: on the 24th, the 25th and the 26th, so runs the proclamation, the curfew will begin at 9 P.M., instead of at 7 P.M.; in other words, they are allowing the children to stay up for two hours more. Do they expect Rome to rejoice wholeheartedly under the present circumstances?

Saturday December 25th

> We that with whims and sects and wars
> Have wasted Christmas Day.
> —G. K. CHESTERTON

Sunday December 26th

The German commander of Rome, General Maelzer, surpassed himself yesterday in a propaganda stunt. It happened that late on Christmas Eve news came through on the radio that German prisoners in England were to have special services and a very exceptional dinner on Christmas Day. Accordingly in the morning Maelzer sent to the Swiss authorities asking if they could arrange for a service and a dinner for 150 British prisoners from a camp near Rome, in the course of the day. It was appallingly short notice, but the Swiss are never to be outdone as go-getters. They opened up the American church in Via Nazionale and had it dusted. As it had been closed for over two years the dusting was a fairly elaborate process. Next, where could they discover a parson? After combing the city they found that the only one who could speak English was the minister from the Waldensian church in Piazza Cavour. It was short notice for him too, but by three o'clock he had prepared a service for the men. They arrived in motor buses and piled out at the church, to the great excitement of onlookers. Service over, they were taken to the Hotel Regina in Via Veneto and given a dinner consisting of pasta, Irish stew, potatoes, vegetables and cakes, together with a pint of wine and a packet of cigarettes each. There was some music, also a Christmas tree in the middle of the room; and General Maelzer and staff looked in during the festivities.

Today the columns of the papers are filled with praise of the Germans' generosity and magnanimity, their kindness to prisoners and so on. Certainly, 150 of them had the drive, the service and the dinner, but in comparison how many thousand Germans in England got their special Christmas celebrations? Naturally the papers accompanied their photographs of the men arriving in the buses, and their descriptions of the event, with the remark: "The British boasted that they would be in Rome for Christmas: well, they have been here." So there!

Monday December 27th

Another German was murdered today by a cyclist who got away without being caught.

Somehow, one thinks of *agents provocateurs* as characters who appear in the pages of thrillers, and there only. We've had a real one. He rang the front door bell, and with no further preamble said that he was helping British prisoners who had escaped and could we give him any assistance in his work. We said that we knew nothing about them and were not interested.

Tuesday December 28th

In consequence of yesterday's murder the use of bicycles in the city has been absolutely forbidden at any time. Cyclists will be shot at sight. Obviously this will throw a greater strain than ever on the already overworked tram service, and will cause real hardship to those who depended entirely on that means of locomotion.

At about 12 today we heard heavy bombing in the distance. Some slum-suburbs of the city were hit, lying as they do near the railroads. Pietralata, Via Appia Nuova, Centocelle, the Garba-

[78]

tella and Tor Marancia all suffered; there were a good many casualties and some damage to houses. They got the railway in several places and the airfield at Centocelle, but nothing can ever accustom one to the sadness of civilian casualties. It is horrible.

The 5th army has gained some more heights near Cassino. But we aren't advancing much, apparently. Here we are at the end of the year, and last September we thought that it was going to be all we could do to bear with this German occupation for two or three weeks. Will it ever end?

Wednesday December 29th

There has been a lot of talk since the raid on the three extra-territorial religious houses, and Fascist propaganda has tried to whip the matter up into a scandal, professing horror that priests should hide "traitors," and so on. But the propaganda fell flat, and will probably be killed outright by an article, aimed straight at the Fascists, which was published today in the *Osservatore Romano,* a courageous paper, if ever there was one. And, as the Germans really control everything here, it is significant that no dire consequences followed, such as the suppression of the edition with the article, or its being torn from the hands of readers in the streets, as happened in May, 1940, just before Italy entered the war. It looks as if the Germans were not sorry that the Fascists should have received this reproof.

The *Osservatore* article is entitled *Christian Charity.* Here is a summary:

"With whom does the Church side?" I am often asked this question, sad to say, even by those in good faith. I answer that the Church is for everyone and she is for no one. She will never consent to be identified with any "party." The Pope and the Church do not side with portions of the human race. They are for all mankind, and for each individual man, who, before he is a party member, is a son of God; before he is a member of this race or that, is the possessor of an immortal soul.

The Church, therefore, does not require passports, party membership cards or any other documents. There are no police, secret or otherwise, surrounding her altars. . . . I said that the Church is for no one, and yet for everyone. She is for no one when a group stands for some special and exclusive interest; and she is for everyone, that is for all mankind.

Men who are bound to one special group or party will not understand what I have just said. They will not understand, for example, that anyone (be his opinions utterly divergent) may go to the house of a Catholic priest to find hospitality there. They will not understand that priests have room even for their enemies, both in their hearts and in their dwellings. They may be called weaklings in consequence, and efforts may be made to hinder them from acting on these principles. But if the right of giving sanctuary is denied to Catholic priests, then one of their fundamental rights is denied to them, and, worse still, an attempt is thus made to force the Church to de-Christianize herself by restricting her charity within the narrow bounds of private interest and of hatred.

A law which aims at preventing the exercise of charity (charity being in itself above all human institutions, since it comes directly from God) is more harmful than centuries of persecution. It is a point on which the Christian and the priest can never give way without betraying the Gospel as well as their own consecration to Christ.

"And this is no secondary matter: it is the boundary line between good and evil."

—SERGIO PIGNEDOLI.

There was an added sting in this for the Fascists, on account of their having adopted the attitude of being champions of the Faith because they are anti-communist and anti-Freemason; or so they say.

Thursday December 30th

Yesterday evening a time bomb went off at the entrance to the Pensione Santa Caterina, at the corner of Via Po and Corso d'Italia. As this pension is occupied by the Gestapo, there was a great commotion about it. No one was hurt, but some windows were broken and some brickwork smashed. It might have been much worse of course, as it was only by accident that there was no one going in or out at the time. The people in the street were stopped, and those in the neighbouring houses were not allowed to come out for quite a while. The author of the disturbance was not discovered. The Germans are beginning to be a little nervous over these time bombs.

At 1 o'clock this morning planes passed over us, flying low; they were probably German ones taking supplies to the Cassino front. There was a good deal of machine-gun fire in the neighbourhood, I think it was near the Pensione Santa Caterina, where they are very much on their guard on account of that bomb exploding in the doorway. They are taking no risks, and executed three men this morning who had attempted to murder some of them.

The Fascist efforts to make the best of both worlds would be funny if they weren't so violent, and pathetic if they weren't so futile. This morning's papers published a Stefani dispatch to the effect that Giovanni Roveda, a well known communist, had been arrested in a Jesuit establishment, thus once more trying to show up priests as people who shelter "traitors," communists and the like. The *Giornale d'Italia,* however, this evening, ate its words and printed: "The Roman Radio Bulletin was inexact in broadcasting the news of the arrest of Giovanni Roveda, a report which we published word for word. We have been assured since doing so that the arrest did not take place in a Jesuit house." Then this afternoon after the great end-of-the-year function at the church of the Gesù, the Fascist official who acts as Governor of Rome presented a handsome chalice to the Vicar General of the Jesuits. This has been the custom for some years, and the "Republicans" made a point of keeping it up, if only as a gesture. The Jesuits seem to be bearing the brunt of things at present in both rain and shine.

May 1944 bring us peace!

Last night the young barbarians at play had a marvellous time. Everyone else was indoors by 9 o'clock on account of the curfew, so they gave a big party at the Excelsior, and a little before midnight, being fairly drunk, they began to shoot up the town. Rifles, revolvers, machine guns, anything that would make a noise was fired off. All around the Excelsior they kept it going until well after midnight, and they did the same in Via Nazionale near the Albergo Quirinale. It seems that it is a pretty custom of theirs to "Kill the Old Year" in this whimsical manner. Under present circumstances it appeared to be rather a waste of ammunition.

The papers are full of Hitler's New Year's proclamation. It is very long and says nothing new, using as keynote the claim that this war is a war for existence, so victory is bound to be theirs. Goebbels and Goering followed suit as usual.

Sunday January 2nd

A cheery broadcast from London tells us that "the curtain is rising on the last act" and that we shall see victory soon. Maybe. But the depression in this city is deepening daily. We all had such high hopes of being delivered by the New Year. Strategists say: "Perhaps at Easter." Three months more of this? We shall be dead of starvation long before then.

Some observers say that there is a gleam of hope today, all the same, in the fact that Turkey shows signs of entering the war on our side. The Turkish Ambassador in London has gone hastily to Ankara, and von Papen saw the Turkish Minister for Foreign Affairs immediately after a secret session of Parliament. Von Papen is a stormy petrel, but his political ability amounts almost to genius. Hitler did well to place him at Ankara, for he can manipulate situations, convince hearers and save lost causes with untold patience and skill. If he remains at Ankara, Turkey will probably not come to our aid. Those who were in Washington in 1916 know something of his methods.

I can't close today's record without adding that Hitler and Mussolini sent each other affectionate New Year's greetings by telegram.

Monday January 3rd

"Nessuno comanda"—nobody exercises authority—is the slogan of those who, at the present moment, would like to make a little profit on the side. Sometimes the ensuing disorganization is funny, and again sometimes it isn't. When we went off to our usual place, beyond St. Peter's, to get a little wine—no, nothing exciting, just plain Frascati—we found that we did not have to trouble about going on afterward to the customs office, as we always used to, in order to pay duty on what we had bought. The cellar to which we have access is hollowed out under the Janiculum; it looks like something on the stage and it smells of old-fashioned cider and mice. A long line of casks stretches away before you and loses itself in the shadows beneath the vault. A little old man in overalls presides over the casks, most of them empty by now. He is particular about his job, and when he has filled your *fiaschi*—you bring your own of course—he sits down at a rickety table between a pile of planks and a dusty wheel-barrow and makes out your bill in purple ink, shaking sand over it to dry it. We asked about paying the duty as usual. "You don't need to go to the office this time," he said, "*nessuno comanda*, no one gives orders any more." But we noticed that what would have been paid to the customs had gone down in that purple ink on our bill.

War is hard on the wine merchants. One of them said to us: "You understand, I am not going to run the risk of having a million lire worth of bottled Marsala or Moscato struck by a stray bomb on the railway." And that is why there isn't any, the Germans having polished off the already existing stocks.

Tuesday January 4th

There is quite a lot of firing in the distance today. In fact, now it is heard both by day and by night, and at each thud one wonders if it couldn't possibly mean that the Allies are landing near here.

Two minor German achievements today. They have given permission for tricycles to be used in delivering goods between 6 A.M. and 5 P.M., and a bicycle with a cumbersome trailer will also count as a tricycle. When you come to think of it, it has three wheels, so it is a tricycle after all. In their thoroughness the Germans are accustomed to split hairs, and we are getting used to it.

Secondly they surrounded and cleared everything from a small but well known lingerie and woollen goods shop in Via Tritone called Nido Rosa. A crowd gathered while the contents were being loaded onto a lorry, but they did not dare express their indignation openly.

Wednesday January 5th

More books and art treasures have been brought here; they are from the Museum and Library of Naples. Many of them had been sent to Teano for safe keeping, but when the fighting drew too near, they were brought to Rome. About six hundred cases were delivered at Palazzo Venezia, where they will be temporarily. As soon as time allows some will go to the Sapienza, former seat of the University of Rome, and some to the Vatican.

Fascists have entered another religious house: this time it was a Franciscan convent, where they arrested General Caracciolo di Feroleto, who commanded an army of thirty divisions before September 8th, and as he was one of those who accepted the armistice, the Fascists have been trying to find him ever since. It is feared that he may have been shot.

Thursday January 6th

Feast of the Epiphany. The Palatine Guard was reviewed this morning. There are about two thousand of them, including the new recruits. They paraded to the Hall of Benedictions, the largest in the Vatican Palace, where they heard Mass celebrated by Monsignore Castellani. The commander, Conte Cantuti di Castelvetri, and the officers occupied special places near the altar. During the sermon the preacher reminded the newcomers of the honour conferred on them in being permitted to serve as bodyguard to the Sovereign Pontiff. After Mass they went to the Cortile del Belvedere, where they were reviewed by Monsignore Tardini, Secretary of the Congregation for Extraordinary Ecclesiastical Affairs, who is also their chaplain. In his address he welcomed the new recruits and reminded them of the noble traditions of loyalty, discipline and fidelity maintained by the regiment. The recruits were then sworn in and marched past the saluting base. A number of the Vatican diplomats came to look on. It was an inspiring sight as well as a historic occasion, because from five hundred they have now been increased to two thousand.

Friday January 7th

Another clothing shop was entered this morning. It was in Via Volturno, which leads from the Ministry of Finance to the station. This time the crowd was less indignant against the Germans than as against the proprietor who, unfortunately, was a Jew and who had held his goods back until prices should rise, refusing to sell and pretending that he had not got them. Someone reported him to the Germans and they arrived in force with a truck, delighted to punish a Jew and at the same time get hold of more stuff.

There is a sinister sound about the announcement that the trial of those who dared to vote against Mussolini at the meeting of the Fascist Grand Council on July 24th is to begin tomorrow at Verona. The neo-Fascists are out for revenge, the fiercer the better.

Saturday January 8th

Some interesting statistics have come our way. There are at present four hundred escaped British prisoners in Rome; they are lodged and looked after very thoroughly, and each one receives a hundred lire a day. Even now, one cannot or rather should not give the names of those who are concerned in this splendid organization, which has its office with card indexes of the men, its assistants and its collecting agents. There are also a few escaped British prisoners in the Vatican City. One of them is an airman who bailed out in the fields beyond Rome, walked toward the city, saw a great dome in an area enclosed by walls, concluded that it was St. Peter's, climbed over the wall and delightedly reported himself to the British Minister.

Sunday January 9th

German civilians have been told to leave. They are to go on the 16th. Why? Is it possible that they expect the Allies to enter Rome soon?

[85]

The feverishly fervent Fascists of the Farinacci type have asked Mussolini to make an address in his old way to the Italian people, to rouse them from torpor and to get their support for the "Republic." Il Duce has made terrible mistakes, but, for all that, he is intelligent. His answer was brief: "Does a dead man make an appeal to forty-five million decaying corpses?" He is living in a villa on Lake Garda, surrounded by S.S. men. They are ostensibly there to do him honour, but also possibly to see that he stays where Hitler wants him to stay. He appears sometimes in the weekly news reels, though it is hard to understand why he allows movies to be made of him. He looks a broken man, with bent head and dejected bearing, much thinner and more lined than he was last summer. The course of events, coupled with his illness, has taken heavy toll of his strength.

Monday January 10th

The *Osservatore Romano* published two articles today in close proximity, on the front page, and the significance of each seems to be heightened by the other.

The first article deals with the Nobel Peace Prize, which has not been awarded since 1939 and has accumulated considerably, amounting now to 618,000 Swedish crowns. Should Sweden oppose the award in 1944, the stipulated five years will have elapsed without anyone receiving it, and both capital and interest will go to the heirs of the Nobel family. Naturally, the *Osservatore* makes no mention of what must be in the minds of many, that if the prize is given for effort rather than for success, then it should most certainly be awarded to Pope Pius XII, for his efforts to bring about peace have been and are continuous, executed by his many diplomatic agents in all countries.

The second article is a strong protest against the Fascist and German practice of shooting "hostages" as a punishment for murder. Before power politics prevailed hostages were entitled to humane treatment and enjoyed diplomatic immunity; they were held by one side as a guarantee of the good faith of the opposing side. Today they are simply a group of defenceless and innocent persons executed in retaliation for the murder of one individual. International law lays down the inviolability of honour, of family rights, of human life, of private property, and forbids collective punishment for individual crimes. These collective punishments of today in their magnitude and cruelty merely add fuel to the flames of vindictiveness, and weight to an avalanche of human lives. The article concludes:

In this land of ours, where Roman law originated and where chivalry was at home, some of us are ready to proclaim the utility of crime as a punishment for crime, and of butchery for butchery. Those who do this are neither genuine Italians nor Christians.

Tuesday January 11th

A special reward is offered to the first person who reports a grounded plane, whether a German or an Allied one. The sum advertised is 300 lire. At the present rate of exchange that would be about fifteen shillings, or three dollars. They must be expecting numbers of planes to come down near Rome, if they can put the price as low as that. At current black market rates it would buy a pound and a half of butter, or two quarts of olive oil.

Wednesday January 12th

Ciano is dead. They shot him as a traitor yesterday morning. The news came from Verona today. Whatever animosity may have been roused by his extremely colourful career, there is nothing but sympathy now, for him and for his family; sympathy coupled with growing indignation at the behaviour of his father-in-law and the Fascists. Ciano's wife made every effort to persuade her father to spare her husband's life, but Mussolini was adamant about it.

The papers, after having been silent about the dreary farce of the Verona trial, gave the whole thing at great length today. De Bono, Marinelli, Pareschi and Gottardi were condemned and shot with Ciano. The others who had the strength of mind to vote against Mussolini at the meeting of the Fascist Grand Council on July 24th are either in southern Italy or in neutral countries. They were condemned to death in their absence. Grandi is the most capable of them and could do much for his country in the future. Old Marshal De Bono, aged 78, a soldier who had never mixed in politics, kindly, modest and hard-working, was so crippled with rheumatism that he had to be carried to the place of execution. Two priests were in attendance on the group during the night before they were put to death, and they died as men should. Feeling is running high against the "Republican" Government for this dastardly piece of political revenge. As a commentator put it: "Fascism is going out in a welter of infamy."

Thursday January 13th

About noon today a big formation of Allied bombers escorted by fighter planes came over Rome, sailed majestically round the city, dropped bombs on the Littorio airport, on the one at Centocelle, on roads leading out of the city, and finally got Guidonia near Tivoli, the famous experimental centre for plane construction; it has an important airfield. We saw them heading for Guidonia when they left Rome. The flak went into action, and toward the end, some German planes went up. There were several dog-fights over Rome and a good many splinters dropped in the streets, particularly in the Trionfale quarter, beyond St. Peter's on the left. A few fell in the Vatican City. Quite close to us here, in Via Quintino Sella, an empty petrol tin descended from the skies, but did no damage. There were some casualties near Via Trionfale among the people who were watching the planes. It certainly was a fascinating sight. One Allied airman met his enemy coming head on; the German plane was cut in two, and the American came down as well. In all, five American planes came down, but their crews bailed out safely; on landing they were taken prisoners, of course. One American plane fell near the Rome-Viterbo railway, one on Monte Mario, and the others in open country. To those who had never seen anyone bail out before, the parachutes looked like great white blossoms floating earthward.

This evening we were returning from an errand on the other side of the Tiber, and it was dusk before we neared home. We were stopped by an Italian sentinel who stood in front of some additional barriers surrounding Via Veneto and the approaches to

[88]

it. In fact, the frontiers of our neighbourhood are closed every night. One of our friends said: "*You* live in Germany." The sentinel was surprisingly courteous and when we hesitated as to exactly what détour we should make, he waved us on and said "*Possono passare*"—"Go through just the same." The P.A.I. is not only an efficient police corps, but fully half its officers are pro-Ally, and will act as an enthusiastic fifth column when the Allies get here.

Friday January 14th

Somewhere in North Italy the "Council of Ministers" has met and decreed that there is to be a general socialization of industry. They don't go so far as to speak of national socialism exactly, but they hold out to the workers alluring plans of co-operation and joint management. This is hailed by our German-controlled press as a glorious and epoch-making innovation. The Roman press, by the way, consists practically of German papers written in Italian and bearing the former Italian names as camouflage. There is always the one shining exception in the Vatican paper, *Osservatore Romano*.

It is a pity that, with the present shortage of paper, the Germans let themselves go with such a profusion of posters. Today the famous Todt road-building organization has plastered the walls with big placards, bearing, on a black background, vituperation of the Allies and an exhortation to join up for work. Everything is promised: excellent food, wages, lodging, ease of mind for your family because your wages will make for their comfort; and work in Italy. This last is significant, showing that they know the horror that Italians have of being sent to join the rest of the slaves in Germany. So you will have everything of the best in the best of worlds, if you sign on. Long-faced groups stood about listlessly reading these manifestoes, indifferent to their cheery persuasiveness.

Saturday January 15th

London broadcasts today that the Allies are making ready to break through the "Gustav" line, which is said to be impregnable.

Cassino is one of the hinges of this line. It is almost too good to be true. Can they really manage to smash these defences?

Up in North Italy the patriots have already killed one of the eight judges who condemned the Grand Council Fascists to death: they capsized his motor car. They apparently agreed with Macbeth that 'twere well it were done quickly; though nothing can ever justify murder. The other seven judges have each received a miniature coffin as a sign that they too will meet death at the hands of the patriots.

Sunday January 16th

The Germans have removed their offices from the Quirinal Hotel, the Excelsior and the Flora, and have transferred them to the handsome modern building in the Corso d'Italia which was originally intended for the Fascist Agricultural Federation. They have erected more of those white wooden barriers, which vaguely suggest a horse show, across the road on both sides at some distance from their new headquarters, and they have also brought a few armoured cars with machine guns to be pointed down the side streets. Thus, still more of our little frontiers are closed at night in this part of town. If they are so thoroughly settled in Rome, what truth can there be in this new rumour that they are sending no more reinforcements south?

A howl is now going up from the press because the Allies don't seem to consider Rome as an open city, having flown over it, and fought over it too, on Thursday. And the worst feature of this non-recognition is, of course, that it follows the German declaration that it *is* an open city. "But the German Command has *said* that it is an open city, and what more could anyone expect or ask for in the way of proof?" They get quite hysterical with indignation. And all the time Rome is full to bursting with Germans, their arms and ammunition, their tanks, their supply dumps and their loaded trains in all the stations. Everybody knows it. Rome is their big centre on the way to and from the southern front. All roads lead to Rome now, with a vengeance. And yet they screech and moan about the perfidious enemy who will not take their word for it that Rome is a completely open city. "But we *said* it was!"

Yesterday, it seems, our airmen got the big viaduct at Orte which they had been trying to hit for some time. This will hang up the southward-bound traffic for three months at least, as Orte is one of the most important railway junctions in central Italy, where lines from east and west meet to converge on Rome.

Pope Pius XII is doing today what Gregory VII did in the eleventh century, and Innocent III and Gregory IX in the thirteenth century to save Rome in time of famine. He is helping to feed the city, and for this purpose has got together a fleet of heavy trucks with trailers which will scour Umbria, Tuscany and the Marches for flour and foodstuffs for the Romans, who by this time are pretty hungry. The Vatican colours are conspicuously painted on the sides and bonnets of the trucks, and expert drivers have been engaged. In the Cortile della Pigna, in the Vatican, enormous garages have been hastily run up to house the trucks between trips. The *Governatorato* of Rome is immensely relieved at this unexpected help given by the Holy See. They have next to no trucks left them by the Germans, and next to no petrol for the few they have. The Germans make a show of anxiety to help all they can with the food problem, and the papers tell of meeting after meeting which they hold in conjunction with the local authorities. In the meantime they take food coming into the city for themselves. They lie first and steal afterward.

There reached Rome today the first copy of a new weekly called *Crociata Italica* (Italian Crusade). It is published in Cremona, seat of the "Fascist Social Republic," and its editor is a priest who, on account of his connection with it, has been suspended *a divinis* by the Bishop of the diocese, Mgr. Giovanni Cazzani. The paper represents Farinacci's effort to harness Catholics to the neo-Fascist party, and, under the sounding title of a crusade, to rally those who care more for religion than for politics, by giving them a political religion. Here are a few extracts from a front-page article:

Fascist teaching closely resembles the ideas of the greatest Catholic thinkers [*which ones?*] and our priests should therefore be full of enthusiasm for it; they should induce men of good will to close their ranks around the standard of our Republic. This is their plain duty, particularly because if it were not for Jews and Freemasons the resistance of the United Nations would amount practically to nothing. . . . In Germany there are more Catholics than in the whole of Great Britain; [*so what?*]. . . . Pétain's and Laval's France is the traditional Catholic France . . . What other proofs are needed to convince you that this Fascist war is fought in defence of Christian values? [*Quite a lot, really.*]

The futility of the article, like the rest of the paper, is so obvious as to be almost funny. But amusement wanes on noticing the name of the writer: it is familiar to a good many: James Barnes. Formerly a British officer, he is now working for Farinacci. His last book was about Albania and the Abyssinian war, and was called *Half a Life Left*. The editorial, by Don Tullio Calcagni, is of the same tenor. Two other priests who, together with the editor, have been suspended by their Bishop sign articles urging support of the Republic because the Allies are "hostile to religion."

Needless to say, no recognizable element of the Catholic Church is identified with Fascism or the "Republic." The Bishop of Cremona has been placed under house arrest, but this makes no difference to either his principles or his actions. He is a perpetual thorn in Farinacci's side. The latter has given to his party as a watchword: "Down with all priests except the *scagnozzi*" (an old Italian word meaning unkempt priests who wandered about celebrating Masses and funerals here and there). The name is used now to denote those few priests who are devoting their energies to Fascist propaganda. Some of them write in Farinacci's own paper, the *Regime Fascista*, a publication which attacked Mgr. Cazzani bitterly for having celebrated Mass for those who had died in the war, and not exclusively for those on the Axis side. Farinacci's attitude, however, is not of merely personal *vendetta* against one prelate, he is at war with Catholic Action as a whole. An article in his paper headed "We Will Not Forget" dealt with the declaration issued by the Bishop of Parma, Mgr. Evasio Colli, Director General of Italian Catholic Action, which had been read from the pulpit of all parish churches, denying the Fascist press report that Catholic Action was alleged to have urged its supporters to serve the Fascist Republican Government loyally. In this way, Mgr. Colli dissociated Catholic Action in North Italy from Mussolini and his friends. One of the leaders wrote in the *Avvenire*, on this same subject: "Catholic Action belongs to no party, it is not political, it is not Socialist, it is not Republican, it is not Fascist."

The launching of the *Crociata Italica* is definitely a false step on the part of the Lombard Fascists, and will do them much more harm than good.

Wednesday January 19th

The Germans have forbidden all trunk telephone calls from Rome; they are increasingly nervous.

General Gambara, one of the Fascists who followed Graziani, has just reviewed the "Italian troops on the southern front," composed of the recruits from the classes of 1924 and 1925. He made special mention of the magnificent morale of these men, and "their affectionate comradeship with their brave German Allies." Brave allies who left them to die in Africa and in Russia, and who are starving them out in Italy! No statement was made as to how many of them deserted to the British down there.

There was a good deal of bombing this morning in the suburbs near Quadraro and Centocelle.

Thursday January 20th

The last of Mussolini's megalomaniac plans has vanished into thin air. An advertisement announces that they are selling off the building materials on the site of the "E.42," the huge International Exhibition which was to have come off in 1942, to celebrate the twentieth anniversary of the founding of Fascism. It had been begun in 1938, and by the summer of 1939 had been planned down to the last detail. All that now remains is several colossal buildings set in a barren wilderness. There it is, and none so poor to do it reverence. *Sic transit. . . .*

Friday January 21st

During the night the Allies made a landing at Anzio, about thirty miles from here. It seems too good to be true. We haven't many details yet, but we are so delighted that nothing seems to matter beyond the fact that they are there, so close to us, at last. It is as if a cloud had lifted from the city. People in the streets look happier than they have for a long time.

Saturday January 22nd

The Germans seem to be apprehensive and somewhat at a loss as to what to do next. Many of them have left Rome. Won't they all go? Last night I heard the quick swish of cars continuously passing along the street. It was dreary to lie awake, but bliss to think that the Germans were fleeing. Those passing wheels never ceased between 9 P.M. and 6 A.M. There were few armoured cars and no tanks; the motors seemed to be official. All the officers in Rome appeared to be clearing out. What joy!

Sunday January 23rd

It is only today that the papers speak of our landing, and they do so in the vaguest of terms, saying "north of the Garigliano." They make no reference to the bitter fighting that is in progress. "The landing had been foreseen for a long time." "The enemy maintains strict reserve about the action." That is all. We have heard by the "grapevine" news that the Allies are advancing steadily and have taken Aprilia, that they are approaching Littoria and that they have occupied Carroceto, south of Lanuvio. For us, that is enough to go on with. But the Germans are still in Rome.

Monday January 24th

The fighting appears to centre at present round Littoria on one side, and Carroceto on the other. If it is heaviest near Littoria it may mean that instead of coming to Rome they intend to join the others on the Garigliano, and are working southward to meet them. The Germans are putting up a remarkable fight. How did they have so many men available all at once for this business? Or did they rush them from Cassino? However, surely the Allies will take Rome soon. I wonder if they know how, for us, every minute makes a difference.

Tuesday January 25th

Sabotage goes steadily forward. An explosion just missed wrecking parts of the Borghese Palace. The Germans store some of their things there, and one of their lorries was drawn up in the court. The old porter noticed that someone stole up and placed a suspicious-looking parcel on the running board of the lorry. Thinking it must be a bomb, he dashed at it, and carried it to the largest open space he could find quickly, which was another court. Almost as soon as he had dropped it, the thing went off, not doing very much harm. The Germans must have had something valuable in that lorry, for they gave him a reward of 10,000 lire.

Since the Germans declared Rome to be an "open city" the air-raid alarm has not been sounded, but today it was announced that it will be resumed; not five blasts as heretofore, but three, and one long one for the "all clear." But, in future, during the alarm, buses, trams and vehicles in general will continue to run. Previously they were obliged to stop, and the passengers had to alight; no one was allowed to walk about in the streets, in fact you were generally obliged to go to one of the air-raid shelters unless you had already taken cover. Nothing more appalling than those shelters can be imagined: most of them were death traps, flimsy and ineffectual, and they were full of a more or less hysterical crowd. We generally managed to get into a church before they closed the doors, if we were caught in an alarm, but it needed some managing as the churches always shut at those times, for greater safety.

Wednesday January 26th

The Allies are still landing men and supplies at Anzio, and have enlarged their beachhead considerably, having now about 32 kilometres of coastline in their possession. The Germans are putting up a strong resistance, but that was to be expected.

Yesterday hand grenades were thrown in a German barracks and against some German trucks. As it happened between 5 P.M. and 7 P.M., the German Command has now ordered the curfew to begin at 5 P.M. This dislocates everything, of course. It means that most people must start for home at 4 P.M. if they are out. Restaurants, cinemas and shops must close at 3 P.M. The punishment is a heavy one.

Thursday January 27th

Yesterday the Palatine Guard from the Vatican went on duty in all the pontifical extraterritorial buildings in Rome. Each place has its own squad which lives on the premises. They look very businesslike on sentry-go, with their military cloaks and rifles with fixed bayonets.

The Germans are offering a reward of 200,000 lire for information which will enable them to trace the murderers of two Fascist women. Regard for human life seems to be fading out as time goes by, and we are going back to the Dark Ages, only with modern machinery to make our own age darker.

Friday January 28th

B. came in to tell us of a quaint adventure with a German. B. is connected with the railway and has, accordingly, a pass which allows him to be out during the curfew hours. The other night he was stopped by a German sentinel, who wanted to find out who he was and where he was going. B. speaks no German, the sentinel spoke no Italian, so their conversation was conducted in English.

There has been a lot of talk these days about the Germans having urged or rather ordered the Pope to leave the Vatican and take up his residence in the tiny principality of Liechtenstein. The whole thing is a canard. I do not know if the Germans ever suggested it, but I do know that the Pope said to a personage who was begging him to go to a safer place than Rome, if only for the time being: "I have told all my Bishops to stay in their dioceses, come what may, and shall I, Bishop of Rome, be the first to give the example of flight?"

There are great air battles over Anzio and Nettuno. Both bombs and heavy artillery can be heard here. In fact we hear them by day and by night as well. The Germans boast that we are being driven back into the sea, but, somehow, we are still there, and each day more strongly settled in. The Germans sank a hospital ship off Anzio, one of ours; it was brightly illuminated and clearly marked. Its sinking was in keeping with their other activities. What can you expect?

A thrilling escape was made today from San Gregorio. The place is the old Benedictine monastery next to the church of San Gregorio on the Coelian, the monastery from which St. Augustine set out to convert England in the year 597. After 1870 the Italian Government took it from the Camaldolese who were then in possession and it was put to various uses. The Fascists used it as a college for the training of teachers, but since the establishment of the "Republic" it has been used as a subsidiary prison for Regina Coeli, the State prison; at San Gregorio the political prisoners were allowed some measure of comfort, and it is, to say the least, cleaner than Regina Coeli. Six of the prisoners, then, got away this morning. Among them were the former director of the Stefani Agency, the former editor of the *Giornale d'Italia* and Count Solaro del Borgo, Gentleman-in-Waiting to the King. They made friends with two of their guards, bribed them, and effected their departure fairly easily. One of the guards escaped with them, the other was caught and shot. Both Germans and Fascists were furious when they learned of what had happened, and that same evening placed the Duchess of Sermoneta under house arrest, for no other apparent reason than that she was a Lady-in-Waiting to the Queen. The Duchess, however, had been advised that the matter might not end with mere house arrest, and, as Palazzo Sermoneta is built on the ruins of the Theatre of Marcellus and has as many windings as a genuine rabbit warren, it was not very difficult for her and her maid to make their way out quietly and go into hiding. Of course her property was declared "forfeit to the nation" and seals were placed on the doors, but not before some of her things had been stolen by both Germans and Fascists.

The patriot General Gariboldi, who was in hiding in Rome, was also arrested today, and news of the murder of the Fascist Secretary of Bologna, Eugenio Facchini, has just reached us. Life seems to be turning into a series of plots, counter-plots, murders and reprisals.

Sunday January 30th

"Reprisals" was my last word yesterday evening, it is the first this morning. Nine men have been executed for the murder of Facchini.

Another Fascist "special court" has been set up to try seven Italian generals who helped to bring about the armistice: Robatti, Vercellino, Caracciolo, Gariboldi, Rosi, Vecchiarelli and Moiszo; as also five admirals for the same reason: Campioni, Zanoni, Mascherpa, Pavesi and Leonardi.

More cheering than the above news was the arrival of our sixteen evacuees; that is, sixteen over and above our four Sicilians. Of the sixteen, three come from the suburb of Tor Pignattara; they were bombed out in one of the raids on the railway yards, a nice man getting on in years with his two daughters, one studying to be a teacher, the other a postal clerk. The thirteen are peasants from Lanuvio, relations of a maid we had before the war. Lanuvio is close to Carroceto, and in the very thick of the Anzio fighting. They have been shelled out rather than bombed out, as their houses were damaged mainly by the heavy guns of the battleships off the Anzio coast. Their fields and vineyards have been swept by the tide of war, and practically nothing remains to them; but in spite of all they are admirably patient and cheerful. They are glad to find food and shelter and friends, and also a scrap of garden where they can smell the earth, see the sun, and do a little digging. They had been living in caves since the Allies landed. They describe the sea as covered with Allied ships. And oh, how they hate the Germans! Their one hope is the arrival of the Allies in Rome. It is ours, too. We managed to put them all up by squashing a little, but they are in luxury here compared with what they would undergo in one of those dreadful concentration camps to which the Germans are now taking evacuees by force. The latest to be established is at Cesano near Lake Bracciano, where they barely have shelter and hardly enough food to keep them alive. The more one sees of the courage and patience of these people, the more one realizes that peasants are the backbone of a country.

Monday January 31st

The Germans today publish their opinion that, by now:

. . . the greater part of the Roman people are disposed to avoid disturbing the peace, and they condemn attacks made on members of the German armed forces by irresponsible persons in the pay of the enemy. Therefore it is ordained that the curfew will be from 6 P.M. to 6 A.M., instead of beginning at 5 P.M.

Nothing really to write home about, for to have to be indoors by 6 P.M. is almost as much of a hardship. No matter what happens, or who has committed any crime, the guilty person is invariably "bribed by the enemy."

Tuesday February 1st

The Pope has ordered his fleet of lorries to bring flour down from Umbria not only for the Vatican City but for the whole city of Rome. Were it not for this, I think we should come very near to starvation. The lorries have just completed their first trip, and yesterday delivered 150,000 kilogrammes of flour to the bakers throughout the city.

Yesterday ten patriots were shot here, on a charge of sabotage.

The Germans are using their customary clumsy camouflage for their desperate attempts to secure more labour. This is the way they word it in today's papers. One can hear the drip, drip, of crocodile tears as they plead:

While German soldiers are shedding their blood in defence of Italian soil, thus protecting it from further devastations which would inevitably be caused by the advance of the tide of war, the great majority of the population of Rome has not yet grasped the seriousness of the situation caused by close vicinity to the battle front. It is for this reason that measures have now been taken to collect workers who will be obliged to labour in the repair of road communications, in order to ensure food supplies for Rome.

They omitted to mention that they are defending the *Vaterland* on Italian soil, and that their scorched earth policy exceeds in devastations all that history has witnessed in the past. One need not give details, their methods of destruction are common knowledge. They have, for instance, when weary of cutting down olive trees, driven their tanks through the orchards; an olive tree takes twenty years to mature, and will bear for several centuries afterward. As for ensuring food supplies for Rome, they want the roads for getting war material down to Cassino and the Anzio front. So they are starting man-hunting again, openly in the streets of Rome. Yesterday 2,000 men were taken, half for Italy and half to be sent to Germany.

Wednesday February 2nd

Candlemas Day. The couplet in old Roman dialect runs: *"Alla Candlelora dell'inverno semo fora."* In other words, on February 2nd, winter is over and the Roman spring has begun. But the trouble is that it hasn't begun. It is still as cold as in the preceding months. Not that the winter has been as hard as some we have had. There have been no frozen pipes, no palms killed by frost, and the thermometer has gone a degree or two below freezing at night and a few degrees above by day. The *tramontana* wind which sweeps down from the snow-clad Sabines has been with us about as much as usual. But we have never had a winter during which the cold was felt so severely, first on account of the lack of fats and sugar in foodstuffs, and secondly because of the absence of heating. With these marble or tiled floors and high ceilings the cold penetrates into the house and stays there, and no opening of windows and doors on sunny days avails at all toward warming it. One needs to dress more warmly indoors than out. Everything you touch has an icy feeling about it: the table you are working at seems made of marble, cold radiates from the pages of your books, you take up a penknife or a pen and it feels as if it had been on ice. Of course, Roman houses are cooler in summer than it is out of doors, therefore they are cooler in winter, too. You can't have it both ways. Normally, the heating goes on about mid-November and stays on until mid-March. That is the law for hotels and apartment houses which the proprietors must observe. But not this winter. However much one piles on coverings indoors, hands and feet are always cold. Rich and poor, aristocrats and plebeians alike have had chilblains of late, some of them for the first time. There is next to no gas for cooking, because the coal supply is non-existent. For that we thank the Germans, who promised that they would always provide Italy with coal. The Pope has refused all heating in his private apartments. In answer to the outcry this decision raised he said, "Do as you think fit for yourselves, but in my rooms there is to be no heating," and nothing could move him from his determination.

We have a new *Questore* or Chief of Police for Rome. He is Pietro Caruso, another of the original Fascists, dyed in the wool, 100 per cent out and out, one of those who went in for clubbing an adversary in the early days of the movement, when *bastonate* were in vogue. He is full of zeal in his new office, and burning to show the Republic what he can do in support of it.

Giovanni Roveda is on the tapis again. The press cannot let him alone. It is now published that, though he was not captured in a Jesuit house, he was taken in the Lombard College, which is a seminary for priests. The Germans say he is a communist, but he is not. He was a well-known anti-Fascist labour leader of northern Italy, and Marshal Badoglio appointed him Vice-Commissioner to the Industrial Federation, after the collapse of Fascism.

Speaking of gas. We are informed today that gas will be available for an hour and a half in the middle of the day, and for half an hour in the evening; at other times it will be turned off at the main. If you cannot do all your cooking from 12 to 1.30 and from 7.30 to 8 P.M., then so much the worse for you. And what about breakfast? Oh, well—lots of Italians don't ever take any at the best of times.

On the Anzio front the Americans are fighting their way into Cisterna (the "Three Taverns" where St. Paul stopped on his way to Rome), and the British into Campoleone. Kesselring has gone there himself to direct operations, and the German resistance is stiffening, so it is said.

The Fascist press is making capital today out of the leading article by M. Petrov in *Izvestia*, quoted by the Moscow radio on Tuesday, in which a bitter attack is made on the Vatican for its supposedly pro-Fascist and pro-Nazi policy. Nearly all the matter in the article was avowedly drawn from the "Survey of Vatican Foreign Policy" just completed by the Foreign Policy Association of America, and reported by Reuter's correspondent from Washington. But the learned association bases, for example, much of its information about Pius XI on two or three remarks of his at the time of the Lateran Treaty and the Abyssinian war, which were much publicized in the British and American press, neglecting all his utterances in 1932 during his clash with the Fascists over Catholic Action. This is typical of their method of approach. Were they to study the files of the daily *Osservatore Romano*, the monthly *Acta Apostolicae Sedis*, official journal of the Holy See, and the Encyclicals they would reach a higher level of objective investigation. As it is, their survey is, as one critic remarked, a sinister kind of nonsense. They prophesy a period of unprecedented anti-clericalism in Italy; but it is one of the few good features about a generally unhappy internal situation in Italy at present, that there is no feeling against the Pope or the clergy; and there will not be, unless it can be organized from outside. The Italians are an intelligent people, and they have had a vivid experience that it is the secular total State, the all-embracing party machine and party discipline which is the real enemy, destructive of private liberty and well-being. They are quite intelligent enough to know that the modern anti-clericals are totalitarian, while the old-fashioned liberal anti-clericals play into the hands of the modern ones. The Church, vigorous and flourishing, is an essential counter-balance to the omnipresent, all-embracing modern State.

This evening's *Giornale d'Italia*, using the article in a gallant attempt to rally Catholics to the Fascist cause, puts the boot on the other leg and points out that "the destruction of the Church of Rome obviously forms part of the Russian programme. The *Izvestia* article proves that, in case of an Allied victory, which would mean a Soviet victory, there would begin for the Church a period of persecution and martyrdom, comparable to the ancient pagan persecutions." According to a recent statement made by General Carton de Wiart, the Pope is the most popular man in Italy.

Still doing their bit toward propaganda in any form, this morning the Germans marched a long column of Allied prisoners from the Anzio front through the most crowded parts of Rome, up the Corso and along Via dell'Impero to the Colosseum, where they got into the lorries waiting to take them to their concentration camp. The crowds would have cheered them if they had dared, but a man was arrested for giving one of them a cigarette. The prisoners were anything but downhearted in looks and bearing. They make the V sign to the onlookers, as they go along, and the Romans who are unfamiliar with it take it joyfully as meaning that the Allies will be here in two weeks. If only . . . ! They say that the fighting down there is heavier than it has been anywhere since the Allies landed in Italy. The Albano road is reported to be blocked.

General Gariboldi, who helped to bring about the armistice, was condemned to death yesterday and shot by the Republicans.

The Pontifical Villa at Castel Gandolfo has been bombed. If this is the Allies' doing, it is unjustifiable, because there were no Germans there, the Pontifical flag was flying over the whole estate and there were numbers of refugees in it, Albano and the other Castelli. However, it is not proved that it was the Allies who dropped the bombs, one of which fell near the farm, and eleven others in the grounds. The wall which encloses the gardens along the Galleria di Sotto was partly destroyed. The news was telephoned in to the Vatican, and the Pope gave orders to the staff at the Villa to give all possible help to the refugees, and to remove the herd of Swiss cows from the Villa farm to the Vatican, where they can be housed in a building beneath the library.

Friday February 4th

Last night the Abbey of St. Paul's-Outside-the-Walls was forcibly entered by Fascist police under the orders of "Dr." Pietro Caruso himself, and until ten o'clock this morning the members of the community, including the Abbot, were kept

[103]

herded together in one room while the invaders ransacked the building.

At about midnight two Fascists disguised as Benedictines appeared at the door of the Abbey and rang repeatedly. When the Brother porter came, they explained that they had been overtaken by darkness, and on account of the curfew were afraid of being arrested if they tried to regain their dwelling. With great kindness the Brother received them and opened the door. This was the signal for an armed band of Fascists, who had climbed the walls, to rush in past the porter, overcoming and disarming the few Palatine Guards on duty in the building. They then summoned the Abbot and community, and with curses and insults said that they had come to arrest the men who were in hiding. No consideration was shown to age or infirmity. All the monks were summoned from their beds, in the cold, and made to await the pleasure of the gangsters for ten long hours. They forced doors, smashed furniture, slashed pictures with their knives. Outside, in the frosty moonlight, mounted Fascist police sat in the saddle, surrounding the monastery as completely as if it were a beleaguered fortress, while, in silence, sixty-six dark figures of the men who had taken refuge there filed slowly out and entered the waiting lorries, with their guards. After they had gone, more police staggered toward other lorries, bearing loot from the monastery. Others remained behind, guarding the community and preventing their moving from the room where they were gathered. In the morning, as soon as the Vatican authorities had been informed of what had happened, they went directly to St. Paul's and lodged a protest with the *Questore* Caruso, who was still on the spot.

This attack constituted a direct and deliberate violation of the extraterritorial rights of the Holy See, as established by solemn treaty. When the news filtered through, much indignation was roused in the city. The press has made no mention of it as yet.

Saturday February 5th

Things aren't going so well for the Allies on the Anzio front. Our Italian friends are terribly depressed, and say we are being driven back to our ships. There is even a note of bitterness beginning to creep into the remarks of the Romans. They had such high hopes of being relieved, when the Allies landed so near, and they are beginning to wonder how long it will be possible to stand all that the German occupation means, principally from the point of view of provisions. The spectre of famine is a terrible thing to contemplate. Here we cannot, of course, know the why or wherefore of what is happening, as yet. Of the two sets of opinions current, the second seems the wiser. The people who hold the first say: "Why didn't they advance on Rome immediately? They had the Germans on toast." The others say: "It would have been a terrible mistake to come here at once, the Castelli are full of Germans, there would have been a bloody battle in the streets of Rome with casualties to civilians and damage to property, and the Allies would have been defeated—a catastrophe." The latter are in the minority, as wise people generally are. But it must be acknowledged that here, inside the city, we have had our hope deferred a long time, and the resulting heart-sickness is catching.

Sunday February 6th

The press today makes a great feature of the Allies' restrictive measures concerning petrol exports to Spain, but is still strangely silent about the raid on St. Paul's.

Monday February 7th

Kesselring has brought large reinforcements down to the Anzio front, and is there himself. They have also brought up their heavy artillery and a number of flame-throwers. Their long-range guns are shelling the Allies from the Alban Hills. Well, anyway, we haven't gone back to our ships, and we have taken quite a number of prisoners, among them, for the first time, a batch of S.S.

In the city, the Germans have given leave for all to bring food in from outside quite freely. It had been forbidden previously, in an attempt to check the activities of the black market. It looks like a desperate measure; and I wonder if it will help much.

The first reference to the attack on the monastery at St. Paul's was made this morning in the *Popolo di Roma,* which quoted a Stefani despatch as follows:

BRILLIANT OPERATION CARRIED OUT BY THE REPUBLICAN POLICE—SIXTY-TWO ARRESTS—MOTOR LORRIES AND TIRES SEQUESTRATED.

Rome, 7th.—Agents of the Republican Police have carried out an important operation in the College of St. Paul's. Having surrounded the building they entered and found there in hiding the Air Force General Monti, four army officers, nine Jews, two police officials and forty-eight young men who had been called up for military service. All of them were arrested. There were also found and recovered 300 lorry tires and 6,000 litres of petrol.

Tuesday February 8th

Last night the Vatican radio broadcast a sharp protest against the action taken at St. Paul's and printed the same in the Tuesday *Osservatore:*

The "armed Republican Guard" did not "penetrate into the College of St. Paul's"—there is no such College in Rome—but forcibly entered the buildings belonging to the Patriarchal Basilica of St. Paul's, thus violating extraterritorial rights guaranteed by solemn treaty.

It must also be noted that the lorries found there cannot be said to have been "recovered," since they belonged to the place where they were found. The same holds good of the supply of 41 tires (not 300), and of 400 (not 6,000) litres of petrol.

After these rectifications of their statements, the public may judge for itself of the want of exactness and of seriousness in all the rest of the impudent report, with its ornate headlines and illustrations. Moreover the report does not deal either objectively or justly with the question of hospitality given to the persons arrested.

As we wrote on December 29th, the Church is for everyone in the sense that she welcomes all, and she is for no one in the sense that she will acknowledge no ostracisms and no hatred. This is what cannot be understood by those who are bound to the passions of opposing factions, and we wrote at the time, "A law which aims at preventing the exercise of charity (charity being in itself above all human institutions, since it comes directly from God) is more harmful than centuries of persecution. It is a point on which the Christian and the priest can never give way without betraying the Gospel as well as their own consecration to

[106]

Christ. And this is no secondary matter: it is the boundary line between good and evil." Will honest men allow us to maintain this principle?

They cannot do otherwise if they realize, amid the changeability of all things here below, the steadfastness of the charity to be practised by the ministers of God, and amid the vicissitudes of human destiny the truth of the old saying *hodie mihi, cras tibi*, "today me, tomorrow thee."

Wednesday February 9th

The local press, anxious to please the Fascists, and possibly also the Germans, but more probably the former, has risen in its might to attack the *Osservatore Romano*. "The *Osservatore* corrects our figures," says the *Tribuna*, speaking of the numbers of tires and litres of petrol, "but for what reason, pray, should one give credence to any foreign newspaper, rather than to an Italian news agency? Is this paper by any chance infallible? It lost a wonderful opportunity of keeping silence when it wrote at length on the matter in question." Apparently the shoe pinches. The writer continues jauntily: "This paper concludes with the words *hodie mihi, cras tibi!* It is quite possible that the future may have surprises in store for us. Today, however, the surprises are not for us but for our opponents. This is enough. *Et de hoc satis*." Accompanying this effort are two photographs—obviously faked —of General Monti and Lieutenant Mazzola dressed as Benedictines, their own heads being printed onto the figures of monks.

The *Messaggero* reproves the *Osservatore* for ingratitude, saying plaintively that, out of respect for the sacred character of St. Paul's, it actually printed the Stefani despatch on the front page and not in the City News Section. Could respect possibly go farther? (Or ineptitude?) It also says that as the Vatican has not recognized the "Italian Social Republic," it has nothing to complain of; let it recognize the Republic or else address its complaints to the King in the South of Italy; thus brushing aside the Lateran Treaty with one stroke of its pen. Its parting shot is that it was "sacrilegious" for lay folk to have taken refuge at St. Paul's as they did. The Fascist papers also printed a long article from an agency which calls itself the *Corrispondenza Cattolica*, though no one knows exactly why it has taken the name, and which states that no immunity is implied in extra-territoriality. This argument was demolished by the *Osservatore* in a spirited article published this evening, in which it quotes the terms of the Lateran Treaty.

All this is hard on the Fascist journalists, the contest is such an unequal one. They have zeal, and that is about all; whereas the men who write the *Osservatore* have brains, skill and maturity. The latter do not enter the field of controversy without good reason, but when they have done so, they fight to a finish. But, again, one marvels that it is still sold on the newsstands and allowed to go through the post; Fascists don't snatch it from the hands of readers; no edition of it is suppressed. It must be the Germans' doing, for which they have their reasons. Like most people, they have, I daresay, two reasons for doing anything, a good reason and the real reason.

A few Fascists, acting I think, on their own, tried to enter the buildings of the Lateran, but the Palatine Guard fired on them, and they withdrew in haste.

Thursday February 10th

This morning the *Messaggero* fires another shot in the combat. It is headed, as well it might be, *"Sempre l'Osservatore"* ("Always the *Osservatore*"). The editor moves along the time-honoured line of argument: "If I say it three times it's true." He repeats what he had already said and what had already been answered at length, about the "Republic" not being recognized by the Holy See; reiterates the number of people arrested in the monastery; claims that no tires or petrol could have belonged to the monks, as they have all been requisitioned by the Government; quotes the *Piccolo*, which accused the Benedictines of possessing machine guns and automatic revolvers, rolls of barbed wire and an over-abundant supply of foodstuffs; remarks, "As the *Osservatore* reaches all parts of the city and is read by Italians, we feel it our duty to speak on behalf of all Italians"; and ends with the pious wish, "May God forbid our ever coming to mistrust His priests."

This evening the *Osservatore* answers what it calls "a press campaign which recalls those of other unhappy times": "The comments and opinions of our contemporaries," it begins, "were mostly beside the point, and we do not wish to be drawn into controversy, particularly because the matter is clear as crystal." The writer then summarizes the points already made, and agrees heartily with one of the Fascist papers which had incautiously ended an attack by saying that the question of extraterritoriality should have been raised beforehand. "Exactly," he says; "it should have been raised and considered well by those who were contemplating a unilateral act which was both arbitrary and violent, and which should never have been committed."

There is an impression abroad that the Germans are not altogether pleased about the matter, and that "Dr." Caruso will shortly be relieved of his functions on account of too much zeal.

Yesterday a Canadian plane crashed in the Prenestina quarter, near the railroad. It fell on a house, and the three men on board were killed. One who tried to come down by parachute was found dead, but was still recognizable. He was identified as George Dean, R.101971. No civilians were killed, but the house was destroyed.

Friday February 11th

The formidable editor of the *Messaggero* fired a not very interesting Parthian shot at the *Osservatore* this morning, re-stating in different words everything that he had already said several times. His fireworks are damp by now, and they just petered out.

Yesterday morning the Pope's Villa at Castel Gandolfo was bombed again. We have not had many details yet, but they say the damage and casualties were heavy. The gardens of the Villa are extensive, and 15,000 people from Albano and the neighbouring places had taken refuge there. When the Pope got the news, he was on his way to the Sistine Chapel for the Requiem Mass for Pope Pius XI, whose anniversary it was, but he stopped and gave orders for all possible help to be sent to the Villa. An engineer from the Vatican Technical Office, Signor Viesi, the manager of the Vatican Pharmacy, Fratel Faustino, together with doctors, nurses and a wreckage crew set out immediately in cars and lorries loaded with supplies, food, dressings and medicines.

The information about Castel Gandolfo is disquieting, and the damage and casualties are worse than we thought. Most serious of all was the harm done to the Villa of the College of Propaganda Fide, which is also Papal property. It was crowded with refugees, and some nuns were in charge of them. They had just gone to the large dining hall to distribute milk to the babies and their mothers, when the bombs fell and wrecked the building completely. About 500 people were killed, and their bodies are being laid out in the College church, which remained unhurt. Other bombs fell in the gardens, damaging the buildings which are scattered through them. The number of casualties there is still uncertain, but it is more than one hundred. The big pontifical palace overlooking the lake was damaged by blast but not by direct hit. In it were several thousand refugees, as the Pope had given orders for it to be thrown open to them. They had crowded in, together with what belongings they had been able to save. Three and four deep they were, so that only a narrow passage was left down the centre of the grand staircase, the Hall of the Swiss Guard, the Napoleon Room, the various private anterooms, the Throne Room, and the great Consistorial Hall; even the pontifical private apartments were utilized, as well as the state apartments. The Villa staff did all in its power to provide them with food and coverings, and Commendatore Bonomelli, the Director of the Villa, with his assistants, gave themselves no rest by day or night. Among the refugees were some who, coming from a distance, had been evacuated no less than four times, driven northward by the tide of war. The members of the Palatine Guard also distinguished themselves in rescuing the wounded and digging out those buried under the ruins. The famous Vatican Observatory in the pontifical palace was not destroyed, but many of its delicate instruments suffered seriously.

There is something very puzzling about the whole thing. We know the Allies respect pontifical neutral property very carefully. There were no Germans whatever at any time in the Villa. They had no supply or ammunition dumps there. Did they have any near the Villa walls? Did the Allied airmen know this? Or was it part of the wholesale bombing of the Castelli townlets? Shall we ever know?

We are told today that "Since the citizens of Rome, on the whole, deplore all disturbances of public order and have loyally obeyed the orders issued, a further extension of the curfew hours has been made, and it will now begin at 9 P.M. and end at 6 A.M. It is expected that the population will do its part in the days to come, so that the curfew hours may be made even easier." We seem to have behaved ourselves to their satisfaction for a short while.

Sunday February 13th

Last night British planes flew over the city. German planes rose to meet them, and there was a duel in the air. One big bomb fell in Via Mecenate, not far from the Colosseum, and hit a private nursing home, the Clinica Polidori, wrecking a large part of it and killing the surgeon who directed it. Strangely enough, it was the home where Mrs. Arthur Strong died last September. The story goes that the bomb was dropped by a British airman whose plane had been hit and who had to get rid of his load in a hurry. The surrounding houses were terribly damaged by the blast.

Most of the broadcasts from London and New York today were devoted to the situation in Italy, where the outlook is considerably brighter. Mr. Churchill announced in Parliament that he had received a report from Generals Alexander and Wilson, expressing confidence that they will win the battle for Rome. Arms, ammunition and supplies as well as men have been landed at Anzio, and the former are in excess of the estimate for their delivery. General Clark congratulated his men on their heroic efforts and said that the 5th army would soon join hands with the 8th "for a victorious march on Rome and the north of Italy." Is it really possible that it will come off? After so many disappointments? One would like to believe it.

Monday February 14h

They are still digging out the dead at the Propaganda Villa at Castel Gandolfo, and have found 450 by now. What was left of the house itself collapsed yesterday.

The socialization of industry called for by the resolution of the Fascist Council of Ministers on January 13th has been implemented, and the "new social order" is heralded in the press with heavy banner headings and an extra allowance of paper, two leaves instead of the now customary single leaf. Workers are to form part of the administrative and executive councils in factories and business organizations, State loans are to be made, and all will be for the best in the best of worlds.

The announcement is made today in a letter from Lisbon by the *Messaggero* correspondent that the Allies are "very anxious" about the situation at Nettuno. No wonder Italians say that the press today is an insult to their intelligence. London broadcasts that the situation there is satisfactory and that, since landing, we have taken 2,000 prisoners.

Tuesday February 15th

The Allied air force is very active round here at night at present. They come over and throw out powerful flares attached to parachutes, which stay in the air for a long time and make everything beneath them almost as clear as if it were daylight. There is great competition to secure the parachutes, as they are made of high quality silk. Sometimes they fall in the Tiber. One flare fell quite recently on the terrace of Professor Bartolomeo Nogara's flat in the main block of the Vatican Palace. The Vatican firemen came to the spot thinking it was a fire, but the light went out of itself, and one of the Noble Guards on duty took the parachute "to conduct investigations." We conclude that soon after he was the possessor of a fine silk shirt.

The Germans are forcibly evacuating the inhabitants of the Castelli towns, and, as Rome is already overcrowded with its 500,000 refugees, they are being taken to a sort of concentration camp at Cesano, near Lake Bracciano. Living conditions in the camp are deplorable and the food is quite insufficient, but there is no choice for them; a German revolver points the way if they try to refuse. At the same time, stringent regulations have been issued against any more evacuees or non-residents entering Rome. Only registered residents who have permission from the German High Command may do so.

Bombing is coming disquietingly close to us; it seems to be closing in on the city. Yesterday between 7 and 8 P.M. Villa Bianca was hit. It is a famous nursing home, mainly for maternity cases, and, as happened to the Polidori Home, a portion of it was destroyed and the chief surgeon was killed. In the opinion of many this bombing of nursing homes has been done deliberately by the Germans for propaganda.

This morning the railway between the Ostian and the Trastevere stations was hit. Of course there is excellent reason for attacking it, as the Roman stations are full of German material; 250 trucks of it were destroyed. The Ostian station is the newest in Rome, having been put up for Hitler's famous visit to the city in May, 1938.

Wednesday February 16th

We have just heard that Monte Cassino was attacked from the air yesterday, and we hope for more particulars soon. These first reports may be exaggerated. If they are true, then the destruction of the Abbey will rank as one of the major material tragedies of the war. Moreover, it is hard to see what real advantage is to be gained from reducing it to ruins, since modern fighting in hilly country seems to point to the conclusion that rubble and exposed foundations afford excellent protection for machine guns and snipers defending the position. Of course, if the Germans were deliberately using the Abbey for military purposes in order to draw the Allied attack, then their action forms part of their propaganda campaign, and also part of a far-sighted plan for permanently estranging Italy and the Allies when the war is over; for perpetually reminding the Italians of the harm done to their most cherished shrines by those whom they welcomed so warmly on their landing in Sicily. They hope to generate fear and hatred today, and bitter memories for tomorrow.

Castel Gandolfo was bombed yesterday, and more damage was done to the Papal Villa.

Again a column of Allied prisoners was marched through the streets on Monday afternoon; we did not see them, but it appears that they were cheerful though muddy. The weather is bad at present, wet and cold. Poor fellows, I hope they have enough to cover them. They were photographed near the Colosseum, and leaflets reproducing the photograph were thrown about the streets by the Germans, with the caption: "They said they would come to Rome: here they are!"

The great archaeologist Monsignor Wilpert is dead. He was one of the most learned men that Rome has ever known, and his work on the catacombs is comparable only to that of his master G. B. de Rossi. Born in 1857 in Silesia, he laboured and died here at the Collegio dell'Anima. His book on Christian sarcophagi is of remarkable importance.

Thursday February 17th

Fighting in the Anzio sector continues to be severe, and the Germans are showing signs of it. Here in the city, instead of driving about in spick-and-span stolen cars, re-painted in irregular streaks of green and brown, they are now seen in battered cars with twisted mudguards and splintered glass, the whole caked with dirt. Some of their lorries that go through are camouflaged with olive branches, of all things. Olive leaves are only a symbol, of course, but it gives one a start to see them hiding what they do hide in those shabby lorries.

Yesterday we were attacked from the air. As before, the railway yards near the Tiburtina and Prenestina quarters were bombed. Porta San Paolo, the wholesale markets near there and the neighbourhood of the gasworks were hit, as well as some houses in the Trastevere. The Pope was expected to go personally to the places which had suffered, but at the last minute he was persuaded not to do so and sent his nephew Prince Pacelli, together with Marchese Sacchetti and Cavaliere Galeazzi to do what they could for the sufferers and the homeless. With the Germans occupying Rome, it is much wiser for the Pope to remain within his own territory of the Vatican City. He came out in July and August when the city was bombed, but that was before the armistice.

The neighbourhood of the Colosseum was machine-gunned, and several persons were wounded. One wonders why there, because there were no supply dumps nor German barracks near it. Was it done by someone who only knew the Colosseum as a useful landmark? The explosives dropped near Porta San Paolo damaged the famous Protestant cemetery, and the graves of Keats and Shelley were ripped up. Castel Gandolfo, too, was attacked again yesterday.

Corso d'Italia, where the Germans have their headquarters, looks very formidable at present. Not only is it barricaded off and guarded by armed sentries, but in the evening they place armoured cars near it with their guns pointing down the side streets that lead to it.

Friday February 18th

All Rome is thickly placarded today with posters showing photographs of the ruins of Monte Cassino with monks and refugee civilians, and reproductions of handwritten signed statements by the Abbot and his administrator. This is certainly a trump card in the German propaganda game. The few reliable details we have been able to gather are the following: On Monday, February 14th, leaflets were picked up in the Abbey grounds warning civilians (of whom there were many from the neighbouring towns) to leave the monastery as soon as possible. This the Germans forbade them to do, and on Tuesday the air attack reduced the place to ruins. The Germans had placed machine guns near the exits, to prevent the people leaving. Twice the Abbot sent emissaries to beg for them to be allowed to pass; one was fired upon, the other disappeared, having presumably been killed.

The Abbot's handwritten declaration ran as follows: "On request I confirm that no German soldier was or is inside the monastery" (Signed) Gregorio Diamare, Bishop Abbot of Monte Cassino, February 15th, 1944."

One concludes from this declaration made by a man incapable of deception that the Germans were stationed a short distance away from the monastery.

This afternoon the Abbot reached Rome and later was received by the Pope, to whom he gave a full report of all that had happened.

M.P., one of our old friends, told us that he was in the Campo Verano cemetery when the Tiburtina neighbourhood was last attacked from the air, and that he and those with him had to shelter in graves when the bombs hit the cemetery. It was a gruesome experience, and he says that the damage was worse than that of July 19th. He happened to be there at that time because he was helping members of a commission acting for the Allies to secure graves in one special plot for those members of the United Nations who might die in Rome during the war. I do not think there will be many of them; still, provision must be made. As for the German dead, there are thousands of them, and the big contractors, the Vaselli, have been given orders to build a cemetery on the Flaminian Way a little distance outside the city, which will provide space for 30,000 German military graves. Our peasant refugees from Lanuvio tell us that some of their fellow-Lanuvians said that all about the Nettuno sector the German dead were lying in heaps six or seven feet high. And that is first-hand evidence. Another friend of theirs who has been sent to work for the Germans in that same locality tells us that before burial the German dead are stripped of their uniforms, such is their need for clothing for their forces.

Saturday February 19th

Two of the Ministers of neutral foreign Powers who have remained in Rome had, each one separately, a pleasant afternoon recently. They drove down to the British lines near Nettuno and had tea with the commanding officer. One may well imagine how much they enjoyed it. But once was enough for the Germans, who refused to allow them to pass a second time. They must have thought it would be bad for morale. It makes one realize how near the Allies are. How very pleasant it would be to do as those Ministers did.

Last night at about 9.30 the neighbourhood of Piazza Bologna was bombed, and a good deal of damage was done to the neighbouring streets. The bombs were aimed at the Tiburtina station, which was hit repeatedly.

Every night at present a strange solitary plane flies low over Rome and circles round the Vatican City. Some people are nervous lest it should drop explosives, particularly on the Vatican, as it is believed that it belongs to the Farinacci group of ultra-Fascists. It is also believed that the same group, rather than the Allies, has been responsible for the damage done at Castel Gandolfo. It is very easy to fake the markings on a plane, as far as that goes, and in the dust and confusion few onlookers would be able to spot its make. That odd lonely plane that visits us nightly has several amusing names: "the phantom ship," "the solitary one," "*il Romanino*." You wonder really how it does not crash into some of the bell towers of the churches in the dark. I find it rather companionable on the whole. Its presence is perhaps more a gesture than anything else, since hundreds of Allied planes fly high over the city during the day, while this one consoles itself by flying low at night.

New ration cards are being issued; it is really a matter of routine, since we get new cards every four months. But this time the process of issuing and distributing will be complicated by the presence of the 500,000 refugees. The authorities evidently want to do what they can in the matter, for they have just published the address of a new office (another office—they swarm all over the city already) in Via Girolamo Induno in the Trastevere, where those who have not had their March cards may apply.

This process of obtaining ration cards (when they have not been delivered to you at your house as they should be), or of obtaining extra rations for those doing domestic work, for whom very small extra quantities of bread are allowed, or for the sick who can sometimes get permission for a little milk, or sugar or rice or meat, when there is any, this process is, I think, unique in human experience. I speak from first-hand knowledge. There is nothing about it we don't know and haven't done, and it beats all. You go first to the "Delegation" of your district—ours is about twenty minutes from here. There you wait for five or ten minutes, and present your certificates and get them stamped. Then you proceed, by tram, if necessary, and if you feel strong enough to be crushed and battered by a crowd of human beings who have forgotten everything except their desire to get to where they are going; or, if you have time and your shoes will stand it, you walk. Your goal is the Street of the Greater Altar of Hercules, at the bottom of the Circus Maximus. There various offices concerning food occupy the basement of a building which is used partly for the exhibits of the Museo di Roma, partly for storing scenery belonging to the Opera House. The basement was not meant for its present use, but flimsy wooden partitions have been erected, with dozens of little windows in them. Behind each window sits a jaded man or woman, seemingly intent only on disposing rapidly of those whose heads appear in the narrow opening, and who neither know nor care much about the business in hand. Their favourite phrase is "Ask at the other window." You ask at two or three of them, and find that yours is down at the end of a long low-ceilinged place with a queue of perhaps 75 or 100 people in front of it, four abreast, between barriers, and pushing only as crowds of that kind can and do push. You stand there for say an hour, perhaps two, finally get to the window, present your stamped paper, and are told (if it is "urgent" and you have paid a fee of ten lire) to return in two days. Your heart sinks. Two days? All this to go through again? But there is a ray of hope. You say: "Please, what time are there fewest people here?" "Eight o'clock."

Two days later you are there on the stroke of eight, and in the end you do get your card. You have earned it. You can now stand in a queue at whatever shop sells the things you have authorization to buy, you can register for them, and you can return there (another queue), periodically, to be told *"Deve arrivare,"* "We are expecting it." And in the end you either get your thing or you do not. More often not. But without the papers and ration cards you could not get them even theoretically. Sometimes the authorities have a happy thought and change the location of the various offices you must apply to for certain things, chicken feed for instance. Once we went over to a remote spot in the Trastevere, there to be passed on to an office in Corso Vittorio Emanuele near the Stadium of Domitian, there to be passed on to an office in Via della Pigna near the Pantheon, there to be sent back to the Street of the Greater Altar of Hercules. The places have a fine classical flavour about them, anyway. Organization is not their best thing here. But their patience is marvellous: not at the time, but when it is all over. Sometimes when they have been through all this they just sigh and say "*Pazienza,*" or shrug and say "Mah!" a most meaningful monosyllable conveying a tolerant outlook on a difficult situation. They have learned the secret of co-operating with the inevitable, if not that of efficiency.

Tuesday February 22nd

News of the day is published with unconscious humour: "The Ministry for the Production of War Material has been suppressed." There being no raw material available, except that which goes to German-controlled factories, the Ministry fades out. *"Et le combat cessa faute de combattants."*

They are hard put to get soldiers to defend the Germans and to fight their rearguard actions for them. It is declared today that all those called up for military service who do not present themselves at the "Republican" headquarters will be shot as deserters.

Wednesday February 23rd

Kesselring is re-grouping his forces for a renewed and heavy attack on the Allies in the Anzio sector. And then what?

The *Civiltà Cattolica* has just published an Italian translation of the "Social Code" issued by the International Union of Social Studies of Malines, in which the social teaching of the Church regarding family life, professional interests, economics and international relations is developed in the light of Catholic thought. It needs courage to bring out works of this sort today, when difficulties of every kind bristle in a publisher's path.

Yesterday the Pope received a portion of the Roman clergy, that is to say all the parish priests, together with the Lenten preachers of the various churches and the Church students from the Roman Seminary. He spoke of the topic of the Lenten sermons, and concluded with a strong appeal for the safety of

[119]

Rome, referring to the fact that Athens and Cairo had been spared by the belligerents and pointing out that Rome had even stronger reasons in its favour. As the Pope's utterances on these occasions have a public character, his words were in reality a direct appeal to both sides to spare the Vatican City and the whole city of Rome.

A very heavy German self-propelled gun was driven slowly through the streets today, whether to impress us all or for convenience it is hard to say. It was a startling sight, with its caterpillar wheels slithering on the smooth pavement; it made a noise that drowned all other noises around it. This is another illustration of how Rome is treated as an "open city." The Germans seem to think that all they have to do is to *say* it is an open city and then rage because it is not formally recognized as such by the Allies.

Thursday February 24th

Today the people who had not received their food cards began to assemble in Via Girolamo Induno, where, as I noted on Monday, the office for supplying missing cards had been established. They began and they went on assembling, tired and hungry and anxious. They invaded the corridors, the offices, the street itself in a struggling mass, so big that they blocked the street and held up the traffic in Viale del Re, the neighbouring thoroughfare. The police did not appear, there was no attempt to regulate matters, and in the end two people were killed. There was an indignant outcry about it, and tomorrow they will have barriers and police to control things a little better. We thank Providence that our cards were safely brought to us at the right time.

To persuade workingmen to join the labour service of the Germans, they are being offered extra food. Anyone who enlists in it this month will get two pounds of sugar, over and above the monthly ration of one pound. But of course the latter ration is largely theoretical because it has not been forthcoming this month. The extra two pounds will be issued with great éclat, to encourage others.

It is strangely cold for this time of year; just when the warmer weather coming sooner would have been doubly welcome.

The mushroom growth of thieves which always springs up under conditions like ours is coming along vigorously. Dressed in Fascist or German uniforms, they appear with a forged warrant to search. The papers publish urgent appeals begging householders to telephone to the police when this happens, promising that they will come immediately. Of course it is hard on the Germans and the "Republicans" to have all this competition in the stealing business.

Placards on the walls gain in quantity though steadily losing in size and intelligence. Pictures of starving children deported to Russia are supposed to convince passers-by that that is what will happen to their children if the Allies win the war, and induce them to rush to enlist in the Republican forces. There is another quite amusing one, though it is got up in the style of the 1890's, and is small and badly printed. There are four oblong medallions on it of Cavour, Mazzini, Crispi and Mussolini as statesmen who made the greatness of Italy. Well, the other three, perhaps, but Mussolini. . . . And he looks extra repulsive there in civilian clothes, with a wing collar and a four-in-hand tie.

L.L. came in this afternoon to say good-bye, as she is going to Milan. What she told us would be past belief unless it were not being done by the Germans, and is on a par with what they have done elsewhere. L. had been with her brother, who speaks German admirably, to try to obtain the release of an unfortunate man who had been arrested by the German S.S. and taken to Via Tasso. That is just the name of a street, over in the direction of Santa Croce, but today "Via Tasso" stands for all the horrors of systematic torture. Officially, it is the Gestapo temporary prison located in that street, in reality it is a place whence very few return and when they do so they are often broken men. Those who do not return are either tortured to death or shot. Names of accomplices and confederates are forced from the victims unless they have superhuman endurance. When they die their families are often not told, for mental cruelty as well as physical is brought to a fine art by the Germans. The man whom L. and her brother were trying to rescue had been ill-treated immediately

[121]

on arrival, for another friend who went there said that the prisoner had no teeth and that when he entered the hall where they question prisoners there were teeth scattered about on the floor. The worst of the S.S. in Via Tasso is a huge man known as "the giant." His methods are those practised at Dachau and at other famous German concentration camps. He is so cruel that even the other S.S. men on duty can't stand it and sometimes shout to him to stop tormenting his victim. A young officer at the door, who receives enquirers, is horribly polite and smiling, pretends to look up names in his book, then sends distraught wives and mothers off on wild-goose chases to places such as the political department of the Roman prison of Regina Coeli, or San Gregorio, when all the time the man they are seeking is either there helpless in a cell, or has been shot. The few who are released are forced to swear secrecy about everything that has passed. The officer in command is called Wolff. His name will probably figure prominently on the lists of criminals brought to trial in the local post-war courts. He will need an efficient bodyguard before execution, as otherwise he would be torn in pieces by the Roman people.

Saturday February 26th

Heavy artillery duels at Anzio, which we hear in the city, come from Kesselring's latest attempt to drive us into the sea. They say that the Grenadier Guards have distinguished themselves greatly in holding our positions down there.

Sunday February 27th

Memories of the Battle of Cannae, of Hannibal threatening Rome, of the centuries which from the Capitol look down on the Eternal City, of Garibaldi, of everything in short which lends itself to an appeal to join up, blaze from the walls in every part of Rome. The joining up means, of course, to fight for the Germans and to act as their rear-guard when they withdraw. Also to build roads, defence works and gun emplacements for them. In vain the posters explain that the labour service is intended to mend roads that will bring food into the city, that the workers will get good food and pay and free lodging. There is no doubt whatever in any man's mind that their labour will go to build German pillboxes and strong points, so they do not put in an appearance. A magazine article written about Czech passive resistance some time ago was entitled "The Indigestible Czechs," and I am beginning to think that one might also write about "The Indigestible Romans." But these posters! Stupid and repulsive as they are, they appear everywhere with new sketches and captions, new text and new insults to the intelligence of the Italians. They are readily defaced, of course, but still, scraps do remain. On our wall there is still a fragment of the first poster of all that appeared, in May, 1940, just before Italy entered the war. It was not illustrated, but the text explained how England had virtually lost the war, that the fleet was no good and that she was on the point of being driven out of the Mediterranean. I hope it will still be there when the Allies enter Rome, a tiny detail in the setting, but a dramatic one.

Monday February 28th

We are to have new stamps. Well, not exactly new, but overprinted. Neat little Fascist badges have been printed in red or black, according to the colour of the stamp, across Victor Emmanuel's face; and the Republican Fascist Government is thus revenged on the Monarchy. After a given date no other stamp may be used; letters bearing the old ones will be destroyed. But there is a slight hitch, because no post offices have the new ones for sale.

Tuesday February 29th

We are informed that "the food situation is being seriously examined" by both the German and the Italian city authorities. So we are supposed to say to ourselves, with childlike confidence, "All is well."

I am sure the Germans think that when they say: "Be cheerful," everyone cheers up; when they say: "Hate the Allies," everyone starts hating immediately; when they say: "We are your affectionate comrades," everyone wants to go out and shake hands with all the Fritzes and Hermans they see. Their mentality is past belief. You know it, of course, in theory and from having read about it, but you have to be up against it in the round to really grasp it. Just think, here is another new set of posters today, designed to arouse admiration for Mussolini.

The *"pasta"* ration which should have been issued in January is to be issued in March. Italians depend on their *"pasta"* more than they do on bread, or at least as much. So, when monthly rations have been confiscated by the Germans or the Fascists they are just wiped out for a given month; the process is a simple one, but spells starvation. The soap ration is even more wiped out than other things. We are supposed to have one small piece, weighing 100 grammes, every second month. It is now the end of February, and the October-November bit is not available yet.

Wednesday March 1st

Yesterday afternoon Nello was arrested. He is one of our refugee peasants from Lanuvio, a fine, well-set-up intelligent young fellow, with a wife and a baby two and a half years old. He was stopped as he was getting into a tram and taken to the police station. He managed to get a phone message to us to tell his wife to go down to him with some food, as they give nothing to eat there. His wife was distracted with fear that he would be taken to Germany, and she rushed off to him. She was not permitted to speak to him, but was told the food would be given him, and that under cover of the curfew he would be taken with a number of others to the 81st Infantry barracks in Viale Giulio Cesare. He had done nothing wrong, he had finished his military service and was a farmer. But Hitler had said if they didn't come to do his work for him willingly, then they must be forced into it. Besides, Mussolini had signed a "convention" in the name of the Fascist Republican Government, that one million and a half Italian workers would be sent to Germany. If persuasion was of no avail, then violence would be used. As in this case.

Today the man's wife took him his food, but she was not

allowed to speak to him; he could only make signs to her from a barred window high above the street. Other women were at the door, too, with parcels for their husbands and brothers. There is no means of knowing what Nello's destination will be.

The military "classes" of 1922, '23, '24 and '25 are warned that, having been called up, if they do not report before March 8th, they will be shot as deserters. But no one reports.

More persuasion as well as violence is being used for this labour service. Moving appeals continue to appear in the press and on the walls: "Italy begs her sons, in this tragic hour of her history, to fight or to work." . . . "If they volunteer they will have good food and good pay." . . . "They will be employed in their own trades." . . . "Work is dignified and helps society; it is essential to the nation. If you refuse to work you are both guilty and mistaken, you have no civic feeling, you do not understand your own interests. . . ." And from their hiding places men smile sadly, knowing the truth only too well. Some Italians say, regarding this and all the other German propaganda: "They have insulted us by occupying our country, but they need not insult our intelligence by thinking that we can be affected by what they print." Again, the posters: "Many have joined the labour service already; others, forgetting their duty as men, as citizens, as fathers, have not yet done so. Our well paid work will help your family; don't let them starve for another day." Starving into submission is, of course, part of the Nazi programme. "There are large quantities of food waiting to be unloaded. Join the labour service." Large quantities to be taken by the Germans there may be—but for Rome, none. "The Todt Service is a bulwark against exploitation." Just what exploitation? "Volunteers for labour in Germany are welcomed at headquarters in Via Esquilino." And if they don't volunteer, then they will be arrested and forced to go.

Thursday March 2nd

Last night, at about 8 o'clock, six bombs were dropped near Porta Cavaleggeri, close to the Vatican City by an aircraft flying low. The extraterritorial Colleges of Propaganda Fide and of the Augustinian Fathers were hit, while two other bombs exploded near the Palace of the Holy Office. Considerable damage was done by splinters, even inside the Vatican City, where the Cortile San Damaso, Piazza Santa Marta and the railway station suffered. It is very curious. Is all this bombing near the Vatican done by "Nazifascist" planes?

Today is the fifth anniversary of the Pope's election, and it finds him hard at work for the alleviation of the pain and sorrow brought about by war, and for the establishment of peace on a solid basis of Christian principles.

He has sent a squad of men from the Vatican Library to Frascati to dig out from beneath the ruins of the Bishop's Palace the famous library, or what remains of it, collected by Cardinal York, the last of the Stuarts (by right of descent, Henry IX of England), who was Bishop of Frascati in the 18th century.

There was a horrible occurrence today in front of the barracks where Nello is confined. Several thousand men, who have been rounded up, were also there, and some of their wives came to bring them food. One of the wives (an expectant mother) begged the German sentry for permission to go in. He did not like her persistent tone, and did not understand Italian, so he answered by shooting her. Some men who were there, infuriated, shouted "murderer" at the sentry, whereupon the Fascist police attacked them. The civilians, who were secretly armed, fired on the Fascists, killing five of them. There were some casualties among the onlookers, and some arrests were made. The Romans are in an exceedingly angry mood about it, but what can they do? After the dead body was carried away, the people laid flowers on the blood-stained pavement where she had fallen. Nello's wife was present when all this happened. She will not be allowed to see him tomorrow, even from the second story window.

Friday March 3rd

The whole sky is full of the roar of motors, the bang of "flak" and the thunder of an occasional bomb. Something big is happening. Can it be another landing?

The Allies have had a bad time at Anzio lately, but today we hear of the recovery of 1500 metres of ground lost during the heavy German attack on our lines. They have now failed three times to drive us into the sea.

The local press publishes a wonderful article by Goebbels, in which he says that, far from hindering German war production, the Allies' attacks on factories speed it up and increase the output, because they oblige them now to locate the factories in such secret places that they could never be found, and so, of course, work would go on in future without the slightest interruption. This really is a true summary of the speech, although it sounds like a parody of his utterances.

Saturday March 4th

The bombing we heard in the distance yesterday morning worked havoc in and around the railway yards; there was a lot of damage to civilian dwellings, and many casualties. The Allies were making for the German supply dumps, and got them, but in so doing they wrecked part of the neighbouring quarters.

Rome has a belt of minor railway stations, used in peace time almost entirely for goods, therefore excellently suited for the transport and storage of war material. The railway enters Rome from the north, and the first railway yard is at the Stazione Tiburtina. Just behind it is the new and populous quarter around Piazza Bologna, while back of Piazza Bologna are more fashionable streets leading to Via Nomentana. Two kilometres farther on, the Stazione San Lorenzo is reached, around which are situated many civilian dwellings in the districts of Porta Maggiore, the Roman University and the Campo Verano cemetery. The next one, less important, is the Stazione Tusculana, but around it cluster the new cheap suburbs beyond St. John Lateran, and those skirting Via Casilina, composed of blocks of nine- and ten-story flats. Turning eastward, the railway skirts the walls of Rome and reaches the Stazione Ostiense, surrounded by the Roman General Market (roughly the equivalent of Covent Garden or Fulton Market), the slums of the Garbatella, the Testaccio, the streets leading to St. Paul's-Outside-the-Walls. The last of the sorting yards is at the Stazione Trastevere, close to the Trastevere quarter and Monteverde, the latter tremendously built up of late years. This gives one an idea of the shape of the Roman railway and of what parts of the city must inevitably be hit when the goods stations are bombed. Of course the latter were full of war material. In spite of impassioned protests that Rome is an "open city," German military stores and ammunition are constantly passing through on the way to the southern front. Everybody knows that the "open city" claim is just a lie, although German troops were never marched along the streets in formation, and as a rule tanks and guns passed through at night. That was all.

Yesterday the Ostiense district suffered terribly, particularly as two ammunition trains were struck, and blew up, causing extensive damage. The church of San Benedetto was demolished, as was also a factory where 250 workmen were buried in the ruins.

The foregoing places are a good distance from us, so we have been spared, but the electric light, gas and water supplies have been temporarily cut off on account of the raid.

Sunday March 5th

Nello returned from his labour prison this morning. Numbers of his companions were sent north, but he managed to slip back to the end of the line whenever the others were detailed off for their destinations. Finally he was sent with a group bound for the Ostiense district to clear away the rubble lying in the streets after Friday's air raid. Armed German and Fascist soldiers stood guard over them, but he managed to scale a wall, creep under some damaged railway coaches and emerge safely into the street. When he arrived here, his family's joy was touching. Water was heated for him, and a meal prepared, and he was made thoroughly comfortable before he sat down to tell his story. The treatment in the barracks was inhuman. The men lay on the bare floor at night, with no coverings. Once in twenty-four hours some watery soup was given them; if they had no bowl or can for it, they had to take it in the hollow of their hands, joined to form a cup. There was no water, and Nello paid fifty lire for a *fiasco* of it one day. When the time came for departure the men were lined up and counted off like cattle.

The German authorities have settled that we are to have no gas at all in future. Of course the fact is not made public. It is said on the radio and in the papers that "owing to damage from enemy bombs it will be impossible to supply gas for some time to come." But that is not true; and there is enough coal to manufacture it. Most of the Romans are thus left with nothing but charcoal stoves for their cooking, except the richer ones who have electricity. And charcoal is unobtainable except on the black market, at twenty lire a kilo.

Monday March 6th

The Fascist Police Commissioner of Quadraro, one of the suburbs, was murdered yesterday, and a reward of 200,000 lire has been offered for information regarding the murderer. There may be severe reprisals against the local patriots, who are under suspicion. From a private source we have heard the text of the Fascist Minister's instructions to journalists today: "Write touching articles on the death of the Commissioner of Quadraro."

It snowed this morning for the first time this winter. Think of the poor with no means of heating food or drink. . . .

Goering has been here for a conference with Kesselring, collecting statistics and information. The latter is in favour of a withdrawal from this part of Italy. He says that this is a dangerous salient in the German line and that it wastes transport. He has had 50,000 men killed and wounded in the Anzio sector, and he is getting nervous. Goering, I believe, is the bearer of a message from Hitler: "Hold on at all costs"—as in Russia!

Tuesday March 7th

Planes came over in great numbers this morning and dropped heavy bombs on the Ostiense railway yards. The Testaccio and parts of the Trastevere were considerably damaged, as well as the Garbatella quarter; the church of St. Jerome was demolished. Most of the light and water has been cut off again on account of this raid. The desperation of the bombed-out families is pitiable. Nothing has been organized in advance for them, and their numbers are overwhelming. They are wandering about, trying to find a roof somehow, somewhere.

During this raid the Luftwaffe offered no opposition to our planes; the anti-aircraft guns fired intermittently.

The new salt ration has been fixed at 200 grammes—6½ ounces—a month. But shall we get it? We are still awaiting the October soap.

Wednesday March 8th

This morning a time bomb went off in a lorry loaded with petrol which was standing near the church of SS. John and Paul. There was a deafening explosion, followed by billows of flame and smoke. The loss of the petrol was serious for the Germans, hard-pressed for fuel of every sort. Half an hour after the explosion, ten prisoners were taken from the Regina Coeli prison and shot as a penalty for "acts of violence." It is probable that not one of those men knew anything about the time bomb.

People who are desperate for lack of coal have begun to cut down trees, and carry off wooden palings and park benches at night, to use as firewood. It must be fairly easy, judging from the amount that has disappeared.

Thursday March 9th

Increasing numbers of British prisoners who have escaped are hiding in the city. They, and those who organize for them, are gaining experience and becoming really clever in adopting various expedients. A British officer who speaks both German and Italian well, was going about disguised as a priest in a long black cassock. The other day he was crossing Piazza San Pietro, when a German soldier came up and asked him how to get to St. Peter's. Whereupon our Englishman said he would show him the way, and not only did he take Jerry into the basilica, but spent the morning showing him its beauties. The German was delighted, and thanked him profusely for the pleasant morning they had spent together.

Between 11 and 12 this morning, waves of heavy bombers passed over the city, and attacked the railway yards again. Great damage was again done to the districts near the railway yards, and again there were numbers of casualties. We could see the bombs falling, and all the time one wondered if the attack would approach the vicinity of this house. Hospitals are full of people injured in the raids.

The general outlook is not very rosy today. The weather is so bad that air and land activities are at a standstill. The Finns are refusing Russian peace terms, and there is a miners' strike in Great Britain.

One of us wanted some sewing cotton today and succeeded in getting it in the end, from a barrow in the street for twenty lire. None of the shops have any left. If you want a piece of work done by a dressmaker now, you must provide the thread, and it is the same with shoes.

Tomorrow, anniversary of his coronation, the Pope has arranged that there shall be none of the usual solemn services of thanksgiving but instead he will grant audience to all the refugees in Rome, as well as to the Romans, and, because no other place could contain such numbers, he will hold it in Piazza San Pietro. Many refugees had begged to be received in "public" audiences such as the Pope was accustomed to hold for large groups at least once a week; but war conditions, transport difficulties and other problems led him to suspend these group audiences temporarily. Therefore all those who wish to see him, hear him speak, and receive his blessing are bidden to gather in front of St. Peter's tomorrow. It is a gracious gesture on the part of His Holiness, and inspired by his extraordinary sympathy with the sufferings and difficulties of others. It is rare to find, in one in his position, such sensitive insight combined with the statesmanlike qualities which he possesses. His long experience in a diplomatic career developed the latter to a remarkable degree.

There was a heavy air raid this morning in the suburbs; we

don't know where, as yet. This house seemed to slip and slide under one's feet, such was the vibration.

Sunday March 12th

We have only heard just now that, on Friday, someone threw hand grenades at a procession of Fascists coming from some sort of meeting. That will probably mean more hostages shot in retaliation.

The great "audience" in Piazza San Pietro took place this afternoon, in spite of threatening clouds and cold wind. It rained in the morning, but cleared a little at about three o'clock, though the sky was still dark and overcast. The weather reflected the feelings of the Romans. They were saddened by the inevitable consequences of air raids, by the German oppression, by their disappointment at the Allies not having reached the city to free it, by anxiety for their dear ones in hiding or taken by the Germans, most of them hungry and some of them homeless; not to mention the refugees, all of them homeless and many of them hopeless. A rumour had been current that the Holy Father would make some important announcement during his speech, possibly of the withdrawal of the Germans. Obviously it was a childish idea, born of desperate desire to be rid of them; but desperate people cling to straws, and even the most impossible rumours always find someone to put faith in them. It was noticeable, however, that no Germans were present among the crowd. A sentry placed near the bridge over the Tiber turned them back, if, even individually, they tried to join the people bound for the Piazza. Even they had realized something of the temper of the Romans, and mistrusted it. I think that one or two eluded the sentries and were seen among the crowd; but they came to no harm.

On the way to St. Peter's we noticed a strange thing we had never heard before. It was the steady sound of footsteps, along the streets and on the bridges, the feet of a multitude converging on one spot. Perhaps because there was hardly any talk and laughter such as one generally hears on these occasions. Certainly it was a remarkable sound, giving the impression that all the inhabitants of a city were moving toward some goal. When we

[132]

reached the Piazza there must have been about 200,000 people there. It's capacity is 300,000, and it was undoubtedly two-thirds full. It was truly a democratic crowd too. A cross-section of people we noticed illustrates this. Near us were: our coal dealer; the Secretary of the Apostolic Nunciature of a German-occupied country; a Roman Duke, collateral descendant of the family of Pope Boniface VIII (who died in 1303); as well as refugees from all parts of Italy, beggars, workingmen and shopkeepers.

When the Pope appeared on the balcony in the centre of the façade of St. Peter's, with none of the usual ceremonial, accompanied only by a secretary and one Noble Guard, his white cassock stood out in sharp contrast to the grey stone of the basilica behind him and the grey sky above. He spoke of the sufferings of many of his listeners, of his work for peace, of courage, of prayer, of penance, of trust in God, of right be-haviour, of perseverance in well-doing, of faith, of hope, of charity; and concluded with a prayer for the help of Almighty God for His sorely tried people.

During the Pope's discourse he was interrupted several times by thunders of applause, and, at the end, after he had given his blessing to the silent multitude, cheering broke out again and again. As the throng was dispersing shouts were heard of "Down with the Germans," and communist manifestoes were thrown about. The excitement was some distance away from us, but we got away as soon as we could, fearing a panic. The noise quieted down for a time, but began again among a press of people in the narrow street leading to Ponte Vittorio Emanuele. "Down with the Germans!" "Give us bread!" they called out. Presently we heard revolver shots, and people began to run. We stepped aside under the shelter of Castel Sant'Angelo and waited while frightened men and women ran past like leaves in the wind. But nothing further happened, and we reached home safely. The leaflets that were thrown about ran as follows:

To the Roman people, women, youths! The city is attacked from the air because the Germans do not respect it as an *open city*.
To prevent the destruction of Rome and save the lives of thousands of men, women and children, the *Germans must be driven out*.

Catholics, Democrats, Socialists, Communists, Antifascists, we must *all unite* to save the city!

AWAY WITH THE GERMANS!

ROME, March 12th, 1944

THE ROMAN SECTION OF
THE ITALIAN COMMUNIST PARTY.

Monday March 13th

Only today have we learnt of the heavy damage done by the air raid on Saturday. A big column of German tanks and lorries was caught outside Rome on Via Tiburtina and wiped out, but the neighbourhood of Piazza Bologna was also bombed and a number of houses were destroyed. Two American planes were brought down by anti-aircraft fire.

Yesterday, to commemorate the occasion, the Pope caused 50,000 hot meals to be provided for the poor of Rome. They were served in various soup kitchens and convents.

The "Ides of March" recur today, and the usual laurel wreath has been laid at the feet of the statue of Julius Caesar in Via dell'Impero. One wonders what he thinks of the military sagacity of the Fascists, or of the Germans, for that matter. He saw Hitler go by in triumph along this road in 1938. What else will he see before the whole dreary business is over for Italy?

The British Government has indeed taken drastic measures in cutting off all traffic with Ireland as from today. Does that mean that the invasion of Europe may be due at any moment?

Tuesday March 14th

This morning we had the most terrible air raid that we have had since they began on July 19th. It took place between 11.30 and 12.30; waves of heavy bombers came over and dropped tons of explosives on and around the Tiburtina, Prenestino and San Lorenzo stations. All of these are clearance points for war material: weapons, ammunition, petrol and oil bound for the Anzio front in trains or stored in sheds near them. The stations, goods yards, railway tracks and vans were completely wrecked, but the damage to civilian dwellings and the casualties were appalling. Bombs fell in streets where queues were lined up for

[134]

water from emergency pipe lines, and simply wiped out entire groups. One woman was beheaded by the blast; the body of another was blown onto a telegraph wire where it hung until, the confusion having subsided, firemen came with ladders and removed it. One of our friends, M.C., who is a qualified Red Cross nurse, told us a little of what she had seen and done when it happened. Her story ran as follows:

I was walking down Via Nomentana when suddenly planes came over and dropped bombs a hundred yards up the street. I rather wonder how I wasn't hit. When the explosion was over I went back to see if I could help. The first thing I saw was a round blackened object, which turned out to be a woman's head, cut clean off the body. The neck was burnt and there was hardly any blood. The people standing about began to bring in wounded, mostly senseless; luckily we were just opposite a clinic where I knew the head nurse. [This was the former "Anglo-American Nursing Home" taken over by the Italian authorities on the outbreak of war.] I went in, and when she saw me she said: "O Mary! come and help for heaven's sake!" So I put on a doctor's white coat and started in. Every window in the place was broken and the dead and wounded were all over the floor, so wherever I trod I either crushed glass or slithered in gore.

I began by trying to do what I could for a child of four, but found he was already dead, so I turned my attention to a man whom two nuns were trying most ineffectually to quieten, while a third tied a rubber tube round his arm. It was a horrible wound, but no blood was coming from it; the man's lips were bloodless too and he seemed quite mad. I suppose anybody would be after such a shock. Struggling, we carried him to the ambulance which had turned up.

All this time people were running in every direction, others were dying, and women were having hysterics and screaming. We unearthed various other people and got them off, then Y.M., who was with me, and I were called by some men to see if a girl in a near-by house was still alive. We climbed over wreckage, and found a child with a fractured skull, unconscious, but still alive. She was too heavy to lift as she was, so I collected a blanket and put her into that, only to find that the wretched thing tore in every direction at the first strain. However, finally, we got her downstairs and into one of those motor cycle things with a trailer. I climbed on in front, that is to say, I stood on a piece of iron and held on with one hand, while with the other I tried to steady the girl's head. Then began the most awful drive I ever had. We went at breakneck speed over every obstacle, quite regardless of the traffic, and eventually brought up outside the Istituto Regina Elena, where I knew the only hope of saving the child was Professor Mario. He was operating, unfortunately, and by the time he was able to come and look at her, she was dead, but he assured me that she would have died in any case.

When we got back to the scene of destruction, we found that another alarm was in progress, and that all the patients at the clinic had to be brought downstairs by hand, as the lift was broken. Some job. However, we got it done in the end, and Y. and I were free to go home. We both owned, later, that we felt queer for several days after.

It was during this raid that the famous editor of the *Giornale d'Italia,* Virginio Gayda, was killed instantly when a direct hit was made on his house; and his next-door neighbour, a well known doctor, Professore Gaifami, suffered in the same way. There was practically nothing left of either house.

By evening a stream of people were to be seen, with suitcases and bags, going from Via Nomentana to other parts of Rome seeking lodgings. Everyone is really alarmed by now, as today's attack struck many houses which were nowhere near a goods station or the railway tracks.

Wednesday March 15th

As a consequence of yesterday's bombing the Blue Nuns' hospital next to S. Stefano Rotondo is without gas, electricity or water. They have had to build an emergency fireplace in the garden and do their cooking there. It is almost impossible to imagine nursing being carried on under more trying conditions.

At Anzio the situation is more or less stationary. Our men find explosives placed inside corpses on the battlefield, so when they go to bury them, they are met with a new and revolting development of the booby trap.

The news from Vesuvius is bad; it seems strange that such a serious eruption should coincide with a war, which already provides enough trouble for mankind without help from natural phenomena. The Fascist journalists carefully give their information about the eruption a Lisbon date line.

Porches and steps of basilicas are crowded with refugees at present, who think that they will be safe from air attacks there.

We hear that the attack on the town of Cassino has begun in earnest, and that Allied bombs have reduced it to a mere heap of rubble. Perhaps this means the beginning of an Allied advance on Rome. The fighting down there is bitter, according to reports we have received.

B.R. has been arrested. This is a terrible blow to us, because he was one of the foremost in giving help of all kinds to Allied prisoners of war who are hiding in and around Rome. Being a member of a religious congregation, he could get about easily. He took supplies and money to our men, arranged for their lodgings, changed them when necessary, and acted as go-between on countless occasions. No one will ever know how much he achieved. He is British, but speaks Italian like a native. If only they don't torture him, now that they have him . . . and if only he did not have any notes or addresses on him at the time. . . .

Poverty and want are more openly manifest here daily, and the number of beggars is appalling. In any crowded street one meets them almost every few yards, some with children, some without; some old and helpless, and some of them perfectly able-bodied. They appear to get a good deal of money from passers-by, for Italians (when they are not Nazifascists) are wonderfully kind-hearted. One gives away whatever is possible in the way of clothes, which the beggars seem to need more than money, but there is a limit to that, as to most things. We have even taken down curtains and portières throughout this house to make garments for them. As for shoes, there is no leather, so they have to manage with wooden sandals. One impoverished gentlewoman who comes here sometimes told us that, as there is no food provided where she is staying, she has to do her own cooking over what ought to be a spirit lamp; but there is no spirit here any more, even if she had money to buy it, which she hasn't, so she cooks with cardboard, when she can get it. We were able to give her a supply of old boxes we had hoarded, which will keep her going for some time.

During an air alarm this morning, at about 7.30, a shell from an anti-aircraft gun fell in the Vatican City close to the offices of the *Osservatore Romano,* causing a good deal of damage and wounding two workmen seriously. Was that shell aimed consciously at the Vatican City? It is not improbable.

The Vatican is in mourning today for two deaths which occurred last Friday among the personnel of the lorry trains that are sent out to collect food for the city of Rome. These lorries have been placed by the Holy Father at the disposal of the city organizations for the transport of food. On Friday, the fleet of heavy vehicles with full loads, was returning from Umbria, and in the neighbourhood of Narni was joined by a number of German military trucks which placed themselves in front of and behind the Vatican ones. The column was spotted by Allied planes and attacked; the German vehicles were destroyed for the most part and two of those belonging to the Vatican; the drivers of the latter were killed as well as a priest who accompanied the expedition. Of course the German stratagem had been to seek immunity by driving ahead of and behind the trucks bearing the pontifical colours.

B.R. is all right, thank God. We have heard the details. They are from the best possible source: the Good Shepherd nuns on whose grounds (on Via Aurelia, about half an hour's walk beyond St. Peter's) the whole thing took place. This is their account of it:

B.R. rang our gate bell about 7.30 A.M.; he was in a great hurry and asked to pass through our garden, because he had some American and British prisoners (four in all), in a little outhouse on the property adjoining ours. He said he was very tired, and after procuring better lodging for these prisoners he was going to "vanish"; all the more so because the day before he had been warned by a friend that the authorities were looking for him. I accompanied him, and met the prisoners who were waiting for him just on the other side of the wire fence. There were three of them (one was a slight red-haired boy only twenty years old), accompanied by two Italian patriots who were taking care of them. The fourth prisoner was ill and was indoors. After saying good morning to them I left B.R. and went up to the house. It was a very chilly day and we all felt so sorry for the prisoners. Rev. Mother said perhaps they would like a hot cup of coffee and milk. I went to ask B.R. if he would like us to prepare it, but they had all gone inside the room (formerly a chicken coop or the like), and a black cloth curtain was hung in the doorway.

Not being able to attract anyone's attention, I turned around to go back to the house, and was startled to see a German with his rifle and bayonet slung over his shoulder only a few yards away from me— but on the other side of the fence. We simply glanced at each other and went in opposite directions. My companion and I were frightened and longed to warn B.R. and his companions. We walked about the garden for a few minutes and discovered a whole group of Germans waiting near the house next door, which, until last July, had been used by a Fascist girls' association. Someone had probably betrayed the prisoners, because until that time the Germans had never searched the property. A moment later we heard shouting and pistol shots—evidently a signal for help—coming from the direction where B.R. and the prisoners were hiding. All the Germans ran to the rescue. Not being able to help in any way we went into the house, and from an upstairs window saw the sad procession pass beyond the fence: two Italians, the four prisoners and B.R., with no hat nor coat, in single file and holding up their hands. They were led and followed by Germans with their rifles pointed at them. The sick prisoner was not able to keep his hands up, and the soldiers continually struck him with the butt ends of their rifles.

They were all put in a lorry and taken to the nearest military police station. On the way they were not very closely watched, and B.R. managed to eat the pages of his notebook which, although the information was in cipher, would have been compromising for himself and for others. He had swallowed them all by the time the destination was reached. He told the German commander that he did not know the men, and was passing when they called out; he made painfully stupid answers to all their questions and gave his Christian name, and the Italian pronunciation of his family name, and was able to convince the officer that he had nothing at all to do with the prisoners and was released. The strangest part of the story is that the Fascists had already tried to trap him, by sending a message that his help was needed urgently at a certain address. To that invitation he did not respond. Of course, the officer who interviewed him had no idea that he was already wanted by the Gestapo.

The two Italian boys who were helping the British prisoners (Vittorio and Carlo Casadei), whose family live on the farm behind our property, were taken that day to Regina Coeli, and were eventually among the 320 victims shot afterward on Via Ardeatina.

B.R. has hidden himself effectually now, and we hope he will stay hidden until the Allies arrive.

And when will that be?

Saturday March 18th

This afternoon at 3 o'clock there was another heavy air raid on the city. The bombs were presumably aimed at the "Macao" or "Castro Pretorio" barracks, where the Germans have large ammunition and petrol dumps. They were uncomfortably near us, but, thank God, our house was not damaged. About sixty people in a tram near Piazza Bologna were killed; at the big hospital known as the Policlinico several wings were demolished; the Hungarian Legation in Via dei Villini was hit, and the blast killed the young wife of a French diplomat, recently married. She was only one of many, but her case was particularly heart-breaking. Via Antonio Musa, Via Nomentana, Piazza Galeno, Viale Principessa Margherita were all struck by bombs. Much damage was also caused in the suburb of Centocelle. A house in Via Messina, near Porta Pia, quite close to us, was hit; it was over two kilometres distant from the stations. That is the nearest we have come to being in the line of attack.

The Romans are beginning to be panicky as well as depressed. There is nothing organized in advance here in case of raids, everything is chaotic.

Sunday March 19th

There is such a shortage of fuel that it has been decided to cut down the trees at Castel Fusano and Castel Porziano, two royal estates near Ostia, the latter being the King's shooting preserve. Of course it fills the Republicans with delight to destroy anything belonging to the House of Savoy.

Yesterday the crowd of refugees around St. Peter's and in the colonnade was greater than ever; they feel particularly safe in the colonnade, so they camp there for the day, only going home at night. I saw several cows being led across the square; they looked quite at home, except for the fact that there was no pasture for them there. Herds of "refugee" cows are being sheltered in the oddest places, in caves under the Janiculum, in private gardens, in former garages, any place where they can be saved from German rapacity.

The posters are becoming less informative and more inspirational; that is to say, there are fewer lengthy printed exhortations and more pictures, the latest being one of the Statue of Liberty in New York harbour rising from a sea of flames and gore. The scornful air of utter weariness and disdain with which the poster men wield their paste brushes when they slap the sheets on the walls is worth watching. One opposite our house yesterday morning was fascinatingly eloquent with his brush.

The rumour that the Germans intend withdrawing from this sector gains credence daily; and since it was confirmed confidentially by a neutral diplomat, we are beginning to believe it ourselves. They say that an agreement has been reached which will be published on the 25th. Even the *Giornale d'Italia* cryptically hinted at it. It is also said that the Germans are maddened by the naval artillery at Anzio, which gives them no respite, and they are driven to adopt some measures which will save their men.

Monday March 20th

Someone gave us today's world news in headlines: "Red Avalanche Sweeps on Toward Rumania," "Finland Fights On," "Ireland Isolated," "Cassino Bombed Off Map," "Moscow Backs Badoglio," "Allies Behind Jap Lines." Certainly "enough for twenty hopes and fears"; we have full sets of both at present.

Tuesday March 21st

And now Hungary. Another unfortunate country occupied. Jew-baiting and man-hunting will follow. We can sympathize. Poor Hungarians!

The press announces elaborate commemorative celebrations to take place on March 23rd, Thursday, as it will be the 25th anniversary of the first Fascist meeting at Piazza San Sepolcro in Milan; in other words, the birth of Fascism. It may be as well to keep indoors while the celebration is going on. Patriots are increasing in numbers and in determination, and there might be a clash.

The funeral of Giuseppe Tufariello, a Blackshirt who was murdered after another minor celebration, two days ago, took place this morning.

The manager of the Roman Tram and Bus Company has issued a report explaining why there are so few vehicles at the disposal of the citizens. He says they have been damaged by air raids, but it is well known that the Germans have taken them for military purposes. Here are his figures: Out of 713 trams, 434 remain, and out of 661 buses, only 128 are available for service. Therefore, allowing for some damage in air raids, the Germans have taken about 200 trams and 500 buses from the Romans.

Wednesday March 22nd

Two remarkable little items appeared today in the press. No. 1 occurred toward the end of a long and vehement article by the ultra-Nazifascist editor of the *Messaggero*, Bruno Spampanato. The article itself maintained that the recent Allied air raids were mere terror raids, for the purpose of killing civilians, destroying churches and hospitals, etc., etc.; that there were no German military targets in the neighbourhood; that Rome was an "open city," etc., etc. It ended thus: "But, in order that the enemy may bear the full responsibility of the harm he is doing, the German Command *will*, in the coming days, *scrupulously withdraw from Rome anything that might furnish a pretext for air raids and will avoid still more carefully the transit of troops through the Eternal City.*" The italics are mine. If the military targets weren't there, how can he withdraw them "still more scrupulously"? If troops did not go through, how can he stop their passing through the city? Bruno goes on waxing almost sentimental: "This will be one more proof of true brotherhood given to Italians by their allies, that, while their troops are fighting heroically on our southern front, their military leaders are anxiously giving their attention to safeguarding the Capital and its citizens."

Item No. 2 was even more thrilling. Carefully dated "Lisbon," an article in this evening's *Giornale d'Italia*, discussing the military situation as a whole, contained the following: "There are certain indications that with the coming of fine weather Kesselring is increasingly conscious of the difficulty of bringing up supplies for nineteen divisions by lorry and by rail along roads continually pounded by the R.A.F. It is therefore possible that this consideration alone may induce him to abandon the stubborn defence of the Gustav Line and begin withdrawal combats [*combattimenti di ritirata*] similar to those he led after he failed to drive the enemy forces into the sea at Salerno." We are all delighted about this; but is it true?

Thursday March 23rd

It was wise not to have gone out of the house today. Friends dropped in this evening and told us of serious occurrences in Via Rasella, and of minor ones in Via Nazionale and other streets. Via Rasella was the worst of all. It is a narrow street running from Via delli Quattro Fontane, opposite the big gate of the Barberini Palace, parallel to Via degli Avignonesi and Via del Tritone, down to Via del Traforo. It slopes steeply and is not very much frequented. At half past three this afternoon, while a detachment of German troops was passing down Via Rasella, a time bomb which had been concealed in a dustman's cart exploded. Twenty-six Germans were killed and about twenty wounded; eight of them so seriously that they died shortly afterward. Pandemonium followed. Until 9 P.M. German soldiers, S.S. men and Fascists with tanks and machine guns, continued shooting wildly at the windows and roofs of houses not only in Via Rasella, but in the neighbouring streets also. All the inhabitants of Via Rasella as well as those who happened to be passing at the time were arrested, hustled into lorries and taken to what is now called "the slaughter house" at Via Tasso, the Gestapo prison and place of torture.

No one knows what the consequences of this will be, nor what horrible reprisals will follow.

Another turn of the screw by the Germans. With explanations how it is absolutely necessary on account of the numbers of refugees in the city, how a more even distribution of available supplies will thus be made, and that it is just for the time being, the already meagre ration of bread, 150 grammes, as from Saturday, the 25th, will be reduced to 100 grammes per head, per day. It will now consist of one small roll weighing about 3½ ounces. Apart from the weight, the ingredients of the bread are fearful and wonderful. It was analyzed by a friend interested in the chemistry of food, and she found that in it were: 1, elm tree pith; 2, a little rye; 3, dried chick peas; 4, maize flour; 5, mulberry leaves. Of course the ingredients change from time to time. At present I should say that they are much the same, with the addition of a small quantity of sawdust and perhaps a pinch or two of ashes, but I am not an analyst and cannot be sure.

This evening the *Osservatore Romano* appealed to all Romans to refrain from acts of violence in this most serious period of the war; acts, it says, which would only provoke severe reprisals, giving rise to an infinite series of painful episodes. It concludes by begging the clergy and all those who can influence the people to persuade them to be strong, patient and self-controlled, for their own sakes and for that of their city.

The writer of this short appeal (published on the front page in italics) must already know something of the consequences of yesterday's occurrences in Via Rasella. Perhaps we shall know tomorrow.

Saturday March 25th
Yes, we do know not only something but a great deal about the consequences of what happened in Via Rasella. Comment is superfluous. The story is a terrible one. No allusion has been made to it in the German-controlled press, but we have had all the facts from a trustworthy source.

At 2 o'clock yesterday the Germans went to the prison of Regina Coeli, and called a long list of prisoners from the "third wing"; that is, the political wards. Some had been there for months, some for a few days; their only crime was that of being anti-Fascists. With their hands tied behind their backs they were taken by lorry to some caves on the Via Ardeatina known as the Caves of Domitilla, as they are near the catacomb of that name. The Germans surrounded them with machine guns and tanks, and when at 3 o'clock the lorries drove up, the men in them were forced to alight and enter the caves. Once inside they were made to stand in groups of ten, and were machine-gunned. They were killed like cattle, with no priest present to help them at the end, no opportunity of communicating with their families. The bodies were piled in a long mound in the cave, and a mine was exploded at the entrance so that there could be no access to it. A priest and a few peasants, hidden in a neighbouring cottage which the Germans omitted to search, witnessed the proceedings.

Today's papers publish a communiqué from the German High Command which runs:

On the afternoon of March 23rd, criminal elements committed acts of violence by means of bombs against a German column passing through Via Rasella. In consequence, thirty-two members of the German police were killed and a number of them wounded.

This brutally violent act was committed by communists of Badoglio's party. Investigations are being made as to the crime being caused by Anglo-American influence.

The German High Command is determined to crush the activities of these villainous bandits. No one will be allowed to sabotage the renewed Italo-German co-operation. The Command has ordered that, for every German who was murdered, ten of Badoglio's communists shall be shot. This order has aready been executed.

A shiver of horror ran through those who read this cold-blooded communiqué.

Sunday March 26th

The tragedy on Via Ardeatina was played to its end yesterday, we learn from the same source. At six o'clock in the morning, more lorries arrived with prisoners, not from Regina Coeli, but from the Gestapo headquarters in Via Tasso. Some of them had already undergone torture. They were forced into the cave by another entrance, machine-gunned in the same way as the others, and their bodies were placed in piles in the same order as the others. The long mound of corpses was then covered with some adhesive chemical substance resembling pitch, so that the remains could never be separated or identified. Earth was thrown on top of the whole, and the remaining entrances to the cave dynamited as before. The statement published by the German Command was untrue. Instead of 320 victims, they had executed many more, some say 500. Before leaving the caves, the officer in charge ordered the Fascists present to arrange for domestic refuse to be dumped in front of the entrances, already blocked up by earth and rubble. This done, the guards were removed, the guns were unmounted, and the day's work was at an end. Rome was beginning to suffer what Prague and Warsaw had witnessed: wholesale reprisals in cold blood.

Monday March 27th

Every day there are air raids in the distant suburbs and we can hear the explosions clearly; but no bombs have been dropped on the city itself for over a week. The rumour about the Germans having agreed to withdraw to a point twenty kilometres beyond Rome so that there may be no more attacks from the air is repeated by everyone, high and low, wise and foolish, diplomats, market women, journalists, bus drivers, priests, shop girls. They are going, they say. Oh, yes, there is no doubt about it. Just a few would remain to police the city. And what might that mean? Well, they didn't know. Then there was the companion rumour in circulation to the effect that the Pope had arranged everything with the Germans; he would take charge of the wounded; Rome would be a "hospital city" only; it would be policed by an international corps, composed of neutrals: Swiss, Spaniards, Portuguese, Swedes, even Turks I think were included. Anyway, it would be the solution of all difficulties. The Pope had ordered 20,000, or was it 60,000 armlets for the piebald collection of police to wear, and it would all be made public within a day or so. The armlets would have "Vatican" printed on them.

Tuesday March 28th

The truth about the victims shot after the Via Rasella trouble is known by now throughout the city, and the people, grief-stricken and indignant, have removed the refuse heaps from the blocked-up entrances and replaced them with flowers of all sorts; the most expensive ones are laid there side by side with the poorest wild flowers. The Germans have refused to give the list of those whom they shot, and the families of prisoners in Via Tasso and Regina Coeli are tormented with grief to which is added suspense. This form of mental torture is practised extensively by the Germans, and only by indirect means have families sometimes come to learn of the execution or the death in prison of their menfolk.

It is chilly and rainy; the Allies have had to fall back at Cassino, and we're all feeling depressed.

Wednesday March 29th

The German Command has published a "declaration" stating once more that Rome is an "open city," and that they have taken a great deal of trouble to make it so; this, solely for the sake of the inhabitants. They (the inhabitants) are to remember that, apart from attacks from the enemy, the well-being of the city is in their hands, and if communists in the pay of the enemy endeavour to attack German soldiers again, the Command "will take what measures it deems necessary." That means that if anything happens again resembling the occurrences in Via Rasella the reprisals will be still more ferocious. The Command has also appealed privately to the Fascist journalists to urge Romans to "collaborate" more with the Germans.

Thursday March 30th

There is a sort of vague, dissatisfied, ominous feeling in the air. Some German cars and lorries have gone, and a good many soldiers with them, but barriers are still up around the German offices, and they are guarded by sentinels with machine guns, as before. Those who have gone outside the city have not gone far, and can pounce in on us whenever they wish to do so, of course. The S.S. and the Gestapo are here as before.

There is a whole crop of fresh rumours explaining why the so-called agreement to evacuate Rome did not come off: the Germans told the Allies (through the Vatican) that they would evacuate, but must keep control of the Tiburtina goods (freight) station. Next, they had asked for immunity for Berlin, and would grant the same to London; next—well, they were all equally childish, and propagated by childish persons.

The masses are angry about the bread ration reduction, and appear ripe for some sort of food riot. There is no bread at all in Albano and Grottaferrata; in the latter town the Germans will not let flour come through, because the men there refused to work for them. But the men prefer starvation to slave labour. This steady lack of "collaboration" on the part of the Romans and the inhabitants of the Castelli has angered the Germans. Certainly, the passive resistance has been wonderful.

The Gestapo arrested a girl who lives close to us, the other day, because she was "indiscreet" on the telephone. There is a body of 500 operators employed at the central telephone building, listening to conversations and reporting them.

There are constant air attacks outside the city on German columns bound for the front, but still none inside Rome. We hear a good deal of shooting at night in this neighbourhood.

Friday March 31st

Further consequences of the reprisals after the bomb attack in Via Rasella are the strengthening and extension of the underground front. The whole thing is better organized than before, more papers and leaflets are circulated, warnings are conveyed with greater speed, and arms are being collected more efficiently. The patriots meet in places like Piazza di Spagna, or the Pincio or Piazza del Popolo, in twos and threes, and convey orders to the members of the different groups. They have also gained confidence since the establishment of the Anzio front, and in some cases members of the police force are inclined to wink at their activities in the hope that when the Allies take Rome their fate may be less hard than it would be otherwise.

As women have played an important part in helping Allied prisoners of war who are in hiding here, so they are of untold help to the patriots. Bundles of papers are taken to their destinations under the cushions of perambulators or hidden in market bags beneath lettuces and cabbages.

The U.S.I. (Union of Italian Students) unites most of the University students for patriotic purposes, and organizes them with remarkable skill. "We must be prepared to face all risks in the struggle against Nazifascists today, as we shall be prepared to work for the reconstruction of Italy afterward"—so runs their manifesto. A number of them have been arrested by the Gestapo, but a far greater number are still at large and are most active.

In order to persuade more Romans and refugees to go to North Italy, where German power will remain paramount for a longer time than in Rome, the Republican Government is now offering free transport in lorries for all who wish to travel in that direction. The pretext is that they are food lorries, which must go to their destinations empty. Quite a number of refugees have accepted the offer. They are promised good food and opportunities for work "in the north."

The *Giornale d'Italia* and the *Messaggero* are almost hysterical with annoyance at the weekly edition of the Vatican paper, which, in giving a general account of world conditions, mentioned, under the heading "Italy," that Badoglio has succeeded in improving food conditions in the south, in reorganizing travel, in clearing out undesirable officials and in restoring liberty of the press. The fact that "Italy" is considered to be those portions of the peninsula which are no longer occupied by the Germans is held to show "stratospherical ignorance," and that no recognition should be made of the "Italian Social Republic" is an unpardonable crime committed by a paper which "appears in a small State which is enclosed in the Capital of the Republic." Nothing touches the "Republicans" on the raw so much as not being recognized as the sole legitimate government of Italy.

One of the hastily enlisted Blackshirt battalions, called pompously *Battaglione della Morte,* was sent into action recently on the Anzio front. Most of the soldiers in it were under twenty years of age. When they reached the front lines, ten of them were killed by mistake, and the rest surrendered without firing a shot. The same kind of thing occurred when the first of the "reconstituted" Italian air squadrons was sent into action. They went up from an Italian airfield and promptly came down behind the Allied lines. In future they will have German observers on board, and more German officers among the troops.

Saturday April 1st

Two more Fascists have been murdered in the suburb of Quadraro; the Blackshirts are making themselves hated increasingly as the days go by. They are also beginning to be nervous, which makes them more inclined to violence.

There is a great deal of propaganda in the press about the elimination of black market centres; but of course these raids on the black market are faked, as the Germans and Republicans are back of the smaller profiteers. Yesterday there was an elaborate mise-en-scène with plain-clothes police and Republican guards for the suppression of the buying and selling that was going on in Via Tor di Nona.

A little while ago one of our friends sent her majordomo to buy some meat in a Trastevere black market centre. Having obtained it, he was on his way home, when a plain-clothes man approached him and asked if he had got any meat. He stopped and made no answer, knowing that he had been caught redhanded. The detective, however, seeing he was frightened, said reassuringly: "It's all right, I only wished to know if it had come, I'm getting some myself." The meat cost about 200 lire per kilo.

The Fascists are establishing soup kitchens in various parts of the city to try to stave off food riots, but the quality of the stuff they distribute is so bad that the poor say they would rather go hungry than try to live on it. The soup kitchens run by the Vatican, and by the Circolo di San Pietro under Vatican auspices, are much better managed, but the numbers of the poor and of penniless refugees increase daily, and it is well-nigh impossible to cope with them all.

[150]

One sees "Bread! Bread! Bread!—Death to the people who are starving us!" scrawled on the walls. In one place I saw: "Remember the crimes of Fascism!" "Crimes" had been hastily rubbed out and "merits" written faintly in its place.

Sunday April 2nd

Tonight we begin summer time, single, not double, and put our clocks ahead one hour.

The strength and impenetrability of the "Atlantic Wall" is apparently such, and its importance so vital, that a whole extra sheet of paper has been granted to the press in order to write articles about it. They are meant to revive the drooping morale of Axis satellites and the Italian Republicans. The patriots say: "Wait and see."

Two more of the Fascist police were murdered yesterday. There will be some fierce reprisals soon, in all probability.

Monday April 3rd

Neutral newspaper correspondents in Rome have been taken on a little tour by the Germans around and outside the city, in order that they may write to their papers and say that Rome is absolutely an "open city" in the fullest sense of the term. I wonder what they will write. One knows beforehand what the satellite ones will say, but the Swiss, the Swedes and the Spaniards—?

The curfew is newly fixed for tomorrow, to begin at 8.30 P.M. and to end at 6 A.M.

There is a well defined pause in activities on both the Cassino and the Anzio fronts. Some people say that the Germans are running out of ammunition and that we know it and are waiting purposely.

The negotiations that are being carried on at present regarding the sale of wolfram to Germany by Spain and Portugal are of the deepest interest to us here; one feels that they can only end by those countries recognizing the justice of the Allies' claims.

The authorities published today the total number of casualties caused in Rome by air raids between July 19, 1943, and March 20, 1944. They amount to 5,000 killed and 11,000 wounded. We have had no more since the last-named date, and can hear bombs exploding in the distance only. There is an impression that the Allies have decided not to drop them within the city limits.

Civilian motor cars, even if they have licenses, are now forbidden to use the great highways leading to Rome, the Appia, Tuscolana, Casilina, Tiburtina, Salaria, Cassia and Aurelia; they are all reserved for German military purposes.

Yesterday a young priest, Don Giuseppe Morosini, was executed by the Fascists for having given help of every kind, material as well as spiritual, to a group of patriots. He was betrayed to the Gestapo, imprisoned and condemned to death, as it was discovered that there were arms and a transmitter radio set among the things he had collected for the young men who were in hiding. The Pope's efforts to obtain a reprieve from the Germans were unavailing, and the execution was fixed for April 3rd. He died like a saint and a hero. Having asked as a favour to be allowed to celebrate Mass on the morning of his execution, permission was granted to him, and Monsignore Traglia, Vicegerent of Rome, was present at it. The latter protested against the priest being handcuffed on entering the motor van that was to take them to the place of execution. On the way Father Morosini asked Monsignore Traglia to thank the Pope for his efforts on his behalf and to say that he offered his life for him. Before being blindfolded he kissed his crucifix, blessed the platoon of soldiers who were to shoot him, and publicly forgave the man who had betrayed him. Possibly because the executioners were overcome by his quiet heroism, he was not killed by their volley, and fell to the ground, wounded but conscious. He begged for the Sacrament of Extreme Unction, which was administered at once by Monsignore Traglia, after which the commanding officer shot him at the base of the skull with a revolver.

Once when he was being questioned during his imprisonment Father Morosini was asked: "What would you do if you were given your freedom?" "I should continue to do what I had been doing," was the calm reply.

[152]

The food situation is growing worse daily. At the Littorio hospital, where we know one of the patients, the sick are not only not given the kind of food which their various illnesses require, but they are not given enough to keep them alive. Two women who were brought there, suffering from shock after an air raid, died after a few days—simply from hunger.

The Fascist troops who are sent to the Anzio front, now go there wearing German uniforms, such is the shortage of material.

A friend of ours who is co-operating with the Vatican authorities in their efforts to bring foodstuffs into the city says that more Germans have been murdered; the Command has hushed the matter up, but is punishing the citizens by preventing food coming into Rome. The statement is quite credible.

There is so much writing on the walls of the city that a decree has been issued to the effect that the owner or custodian of each house is responsible for whatever communist, partisan or "subversive" inscriptions appear on its walls; if he does not cancel them immediately he will be severely punished. Obviously the police had to give it up as a bad job; they could no longer cope with the spate of hostile remarks scrawled nightly all over the city.

Today is Maundy Thursday, a lovely spring day, and greater crowds than usual are visiting the different churches. They are praying for peace and for the cessation of incidents such as the one which took place at the Nazzareno College this morning. All the staff and pupils were present at Mass in the College chapel. During the ceremony a sermon was preached which concluded with an exhortation to pray for the peace and the safety of Italy. When it was over, a young man who was seated near the door and who was not a pupil of the College, called out: "Let us now say a 'De Profundis' for the 320 men murdered by the Germans!" Immediately a Fascist member of the staff, Professor Lattanzi, gripped him by the arm and hustled him off to a classroom where he locked him up, and, after questioning him, reported him to the German authorities. As soon as Lattanzi was gone the boys

[153]

rushed to the classroom and forced the door open so that the prisoner might escape. They made a note of Lattanzi's name, for future reference, and when the Allies arrive, his lot will not be an enviable one.

However, the matter did not end there, for the Gestapo arrested a number of the boys in their own homes and took them to Via Tasso to be interrogated.

Good Friday April 7th

We have had bad news today. One of the foremost helpers of the hidden British prisoners here has been caught and was tortured, and a certain amount of information has leaked out. All the men in concealment must change their lodgings, and at once. How is it going to be possible to get it done at such short notice?

The miracle has been achieved, thanks to the united efforts of the group; the lodgings were changed, and none of the British were caught. When all this is over, one hopes that recognition will be made of the devoted service that Italian patriots and others have been giving to our men.

There is a new sign in German at the top of the roadway in Via Veneto: "Only Generals pass this way." It gives quite a tone to the street.

From the Vatican we have heard statistics about the number of men rounded up in the Castelli by the Germans for their forced labour organizations. They total 8,000.

The Pope has sent 7,000 loaves of bread to the concentration camp at Cesena, near Lake Bracciano, for the refugees whom the Germans have forcibly evacuated. It is one of the worst in Italy; the people there are housed in wretched army huts, with no blankets, no sanitation and next to no food. Numbers of them have died of hunger and exposure. The Pope has saved many of their lives by sending food to the camp.

Easter Sunday April 9th

There is a rumour that the Allies have landed at Civitavecchia; but it is not to be taken seriously.

This morning, in Corso d'Italia, in front of the building the Germans use for their offices and which is elaborately barricaded off, they gave a brilliant band concert in honour of Easter Day. A large crowd collected to listen to them; there is no doubt whatever that they are born musicians. If only they would stick to music instead of making war!

Monday April 10th

The press has given us a good scolding today for "giving credit to rumours malignantly spread by agents of the enemy" but does not say what they are, which would have been much more interesting. It ends by pointing out how futile it is to attempt "to sow discord between us and our chivalrous allies who are defending our land with legendary valour." Those who do not collaborate with these "allies" deserve to be "treated as slaves exiled from their country and outside the pale of civilization." And, it points out, the kind Germans have done so much to make everything pleasant for the Romans—"if painful incidents have occurred, necessitating prompt measures in retaliation, this should not give rise to alarmist tales as to the future intentions of the Germans."

Well, well, you never know.

Even if there is a war, aggravated by German occupation, the Romans will stick to their time-honoured customs. Among these is the "*scampagnata*" or day in the country—*fuori porta*, outside the gates—on Easter Monday. As no one is allowed to go outside the city at present, they have taken what few provisions they could scrape together and have had their day out, by picnicking all over the Forum and the Palatine, and in various parks. It was better than nothing; and tradition must be upheld.

Tuesday April 11th

One of our peasants returned today from Lanuvio, where he managed to go to look at his property. He was horror-struck at what he had heard about the Germans who, on Easter Sunday, surrounded the parish church at Galloro, and took all the men off to labour for them; but worse still, they killed all the men in a village in the Abruzzi. It seems that in this village the peasants had been kind to escaped British prisoners, and to patriots, giving them food and shelter. The Germans simply surrounded it, rounded up the men, placed them with their backs to the church wall, and there, in front of their women folk, whom they obliged to be present, shot them. Virginio was almost crying when he told us of this horror.

Someone came in today, wanting to borrow an English grammar from us. It seems that, such is the demand, every English grammar in Rome has been bought up by those who wish to be really proficient in the language when the Allies arrive. Most of the French grammars have also been sold out, but there are piles of German textbooks available for anyone who wants them. But no one does.

The supply of salt appears to be exhausted, and the monthly ration is to be reduced to 150 grammes per head—provided we get even that much. Cooking without salt is a novel experience.

Wednesday April 12th

The personally conducted tour made by the neutral press correspondents on April 3rd is beginning to bear fruit. The *Basler Nachrichten* says that German military supplies are now transported along narrow country roads which make a wide détour around Rome, thus using much more fuel than if they took the broad ones which lead through the city; and this is very satisfactory for the German press censors. But the Swede—ungrateful Swede! How could he stoop so low?—spoiled the game and spilled the beans. He told the truth, the whole truth and nothing but the truth, and said that Rome was not an open city, that there were quantities of military supply dépots in it, and that military traffic went through it. He also produced some photographs in support of his statements.

The wrath of the German and Fascist authorities knows no bounds. They say he is a liar. They have forbidden all tours for press correspondents, and no one may use a camera in future. But all that changes nothing. The fat is irremediably in the fire.

Marshal Kesselring has visited the Pope again; afterward he paid a visit to the Cardinal Secretary of State. When Kesselring had gone the Cardinal remarked smilingly to a friend of ours: "There will be good news for us next week." We conclude that it means they will withdraw from this part of Italy on account of the difficulty of transport. The hope that has subsided so many times flares up again. But one does not believe these hopeful statements so easily as before; we find that we are developing a sort of protective covering of incredulity.

The increase in robberies is alarming at present. Not official robberies by the Germans, but ordinary ones, carried out by thieves, sometimes masked, at other times disguised in Fascist uniforms. Lawlessness is in the air, police protection is weak, and thieving, as always, is an easy way of accumulating riches. It has reached such a degree that the following notice was found affixed to a tobacconist's shop recently: "Gentlemen who are thinking of robbing this shop are warned that the cigarettes, matches and other goods are stored elsewhere during the night. Will they therefore kindly refrain from damaging the shutters."

Looting "officially," the Germans collected a large number of bales of cloth, which they stored in a shop almost opposite our house. A day or two ago they emptied all the pieces of material into lorries and drove off. During the process sentries stood on guard at the door, in case of thieves, I suppose.

This morning we took a turn in Villa Borghese to see the spring. It has really come at last, and the blessed warmth is penetrating into our unheated houses, thawing everything, and making one forget the months of desperate struggle against the cold. The weather is perfect; mild yet fresh. In a few weeks we shall be perspiring and trying to shut out the heat and glare. It won't matter though, if the Allies are here. It seems almost as if nothing would matter if only we could get rid of the Germans.

Close to the entrance of Villa Borghese were two sinister looking German armoured cars with guns, ready to rake the approaches to the gardens if required. Nevertheless their shadow could not dim the glory of the surroundings, nor change the delicate beauty of young leaves and grass. The colour of the budding trees was like a delicate melody: golden-green, silver-green, blue-green, olive-green, mauve-green and pinkish-green harmonized against a background of thin weeping willows and solid ilexes. The buds themselves seemed deliberately fantastic in shape and texture; they were feathery, knobby, vertical, horizontal, stiffly conventionalized or recklessly baroque. Judas trees, Japanese cherry, wistaria, hawthorn, almond and peach trees made a foreground of colour against a background of lawns and shrubs. The Giardino del Lago, the loveliest spot of all, was closed and guarded. Inside there were piles of sacks, and lorries standing under the trees. The Germans are using it for storing food. Of course the loss of the Ukraine has told heavily on them, and in consequence on us, for they do not intend to suffer so long as they can live on occupied regions.

Friday April 14th

We heard heavy anti-aircraft gunfire this morning, and at intervals the sirens sounded an alarm. The latter have become matter for jokes among the Romans. Sometimes they sound after the planes have passed, sometimes beforehand, and sometimes when there are no planes at all. Either the officer in command is temperamental or there is no particular person to give orders. Most probably there is no one. "Nessuno comanda." It is all part of the chaos.

Saturday April 15th

Our group is doing what it can for Alf and Charlie. They are very special, as they are in a hospital which, fortunately, is not a military one. Alf is from the East End of London and Charlie is Scotch, a window cleaner in private life. They belong to the Barsetshire and Loamshire, and were wounded at Anzio. The Germans took one of our positions, so immediately afterward we bombed it to bits. Alf and Charlie did not get away with the others, and were badly hurt. A hit at the top of the spinal column paralyzed Alf's arms; Charlie lost an eye and received a bad abdominal wound. The Germans picked them up, together with two of theirs, and put them in an ambulance. During the

[158]

ride they were robbed of everything except their boots and Charlie's underclothes, which were too bloodsoaked to be of use. On the way to the military hospital the ambulance broke down, so they were hastily taken to the nearest one for civilians—let us call it the Benito. They were put to bed in a small ward with four beds in it. The German authorities immediately sent quantities of food, coffee, eggs, bread, butter and milk for theirs, but nothing for the British soldiers. They probably meant them to die of hunger. However, one of the nuns on the hospital staff wangled food for them, and pulled them through the most critical period. The Chief Surgeon was kindness itself, giving them every possible remedy he could devise, and promising that he would manage that they should not be transferred to a military hospital, which would mean a concentration camp when they had recovered. One of our group heard of the two men's plight from the spirited nun who had helped them through the first days; she got to work, and now the men are fed regularly. Someone makes bread for them, another produces eggs, a third gets rice puddings, and between them all a little tea has been found. Charlie longs for potatoes and gravy, which are very hard to procure. Alf isn't used to dilatory ways; he is only twenty, and moreover fears bombs. He was in a fury the other day and said to the leading member of our group: "I say, Miss, I ain't kiddin' —I'm not goin' to that electric treatment any more, they kep' me waitin' two hours. I might of 'ad a bomb on me down there!" There is a sentry on duty outside the little ward and a big sign "No admittance," but the most valiant member of the organization, who speaks Italian like a native, simply says "May I pass," and walks in. That is all there is to it. That, and courage on her part. She is trying to get medicines for them, as there are none in the hospital. The Germans have taken all there are, except those to be found in a few chemists' shops. They have also taken the surgical instruments from the hospitals, including the only electric lancet there was in the city, at the Celio hospital.

There must be a big meeting on at the Excelsior Hotel today. When we passed it on our way to Piazza di Spagna there were double the usual number of sentries around it, and when we tried to go down Via Sistina, where the German Transport Headquarters are, a sentinel at the end of the street barred the way saying, "You cannot pass here today," with a slight emphasis on the "today."

Farther on we met one of the most ardent patriots we know, and he told us that there would be a big attack in a few days. He seemed very cheerful.

Another friend brought news of an arrangement made through the Vatican by which the Allies will grant the Germans three days' armistice in which to withdraw to their Livorno-Rimini line. In theory that may be magnificent, but it is not war; and we do not believe it. War isn't a game of hide-and-seek, it is destruction of the enemy. Another British prisoner whom we had the pleasure of seeing is an officer of high rank, and he also laughed at the idea of such a truce. "Find the enemy and destroy him," he said; "that is war."

There is a significant line or two at the end of an announcement in today's papers of a football match to be played tomorrow for the benefit of destitute refugees: "In consequence of orders issued by the German Command, German soldiers will not be admitted to the Stadium for the football match." It makes one realize how nervous they are in presence of simmering popular resentment.

Sunday April 16th

Mass was celebrated this morning at St. Mary Major's for the repose of the souls of all those who had been killed in Rome, by air raids or other means, including execution by the Germans. Afterward, in the square in front of the basilica, someone distributed "subversive" leaflets; a Blackshirt soldier interfered and was killed; some promiscuous shooting followed. No Germans were killed, so perhaps there will not be such fierce reprisals as one fears. Tension increases daily, as the patriots become more hopeful and the Germans make themselves more hated.

That rumour regarding the withdrawal of the Germans will not die. Today we hear that it is absolutely true, that negotiations are in progress, and that they are about to abandon the southern front. "The news will be made public officially on the 25th."—Will it? Our expectations are not as resilient as they used to be.

The horrors at Via Tasso continue steadily. Among the boys taken by the Germans after the incident at the Nazzareno College on April 6th was young Morelli. His parents were in despair about him, and tried in vain to have him released. He has just been freed and brought back to them, but in a condition bordering on insanity. He cannot speak, and shrinks away from anyone who approaches him, no matter how gently. He does not recognize his mother and father, and shrinks even from them. One hardly dares to imagine their feelings. They have taken him to the best specialists, who hold out some faint hope of curing him, though they fear that the brain has been injured permanently. Among the more old-fashioned instruments of torture at Via Tasso are some modern ones, among which is a thing called the "electric helmet." When I learnt of its existence I hadn't the courage to hear more details; the name was enough.

The weather is overcast and sultry today, and to the distant rumble of the storm is joined the rumble of heavy artillery; it sounds like naval guns off the coast. It is one of those ominous days when you feel that anything might happen.

Last night, German soldiers in a house near us which they have occupied for some time past held a sing-song, which lasted until after midnight. It was followed by the departure of numbers of cars and lorries, all of which were noisily cranked up before starting. Someone said it was a sign they were leaving. Honestly, I don't want to *hear* any more that they are going; I just want to *see* them go, that is all. Of course it doesn't do to be rude when people start telling you this, it is the wish that is father to the thought and all that—but why do they raise their own hopes this way? Rome means much too much to Hitler for him ever to allow his troops to withdraw. They will have to be forced out by the Allies, at the point of the sword. However—

Giovanni Gentile, the foremost "philosopher of Fascism" and President of the "Italian Academy" founded by Mussolini in 1926, was murdered yesterday in Florence, by cyclists who fired revolver shots at him while he was driving in his motor car. There have also been one or two minor Fascists murdered in Rome within the last few days. Murder is a ghastly business, and violence breeds violence. Onlookers are helpless. The whole thing

[161]

is a tragedy. Giovanni Gentile, of course, is an outstanding figure in the Fascist world, and came nearer to providing it with a philosophy than any other writer, though, naturally, he failed in the attempt. The papers have been filled with articles on Gentile and with indignant comments on the manner of his death; the best of all was the column which appeared in the *Osservatore Romano,* protesting against the rising tide of violence and murder which threatens to drown all Christian sentiments in the hearts of men. "Men kill each other thus," it said, "because they have killed the thought of God in their hearts," and concludes: "Without God, without Jesus Christ, without charity, how dare we dream of peace and of redemptive justice, if peace with God is not observed but repudiated daily more and more, and if justice is reduced to the blind impulse of revenge?"

Some German soldiers have also been murdered in the suburbs, and the men who killed them escaped; for that reason the S.S. arrested all the men of the district and sent them to the forced labour service. "The people of Rome" are held responsible for these things by the Germans and are warned that if they continue worse punishments will follow. We do not know if any of the men arrested were shot as hostages or not. There is no information given.

Tuesday April 18th

One widespread rumour has been roundly denied today, and that is a comfort. It concerned the Sistine Chapel, where a time bomb was supposed to have been placed recently. The *Osservatore* says today that the rumour is absolutely unfounded, and that no bomb has been found in the Sistine.

The Blackshirts are suspicious of us in this house. They did not come here directly but went to the doorkeeper of the next house, who happens to be most friendly. They asked who we were and what we did, and if he had noticed anything peculiar about us. He answered that we were quiet people, we did no harm, and that in the evenings we bolted our doors early and went to bed. This seemed to satisfy them, for they did not return. Many of the Roman doorkeepers are simply spies in the pay of the Nazifascists, continually informing on the occupants of the house.

Spies have been busy about the daughters of the Duchess of Cesarò, who were arrested in their own house with no warning this afternoon, together with their fiancés. They have been taken to Regina Coeli, and one of the young men has been told that he will be shot. They are accused of being patriots, which is true. They have made no attempt to deny it, but refuse to give evidence against other patriots. They may therefore be tortured.

A friend came in to warn us that "communists will be out tonight" and that the Germans were standing to arms throughout the city. Well, there is the curfew; we should not be out anyway; and if there is shooting in this neighbourhood it won't be anything unusual. I don't suppose there will be a battle in our garden.

Thursday April 20th

We had a remarkably peaceful night. "Not a drum was heard, not a funeral note." The "communists" must have thought better of it, and gone to bed.

The Germans have begun to use the Vatican colours on their lorries and vans along the roads leading to Rome, thus laying the real Vatican motors open to attack. One or two have been machine-gunned lately on account of this new form of treachery.

Everything is relatively quiet on our Italian fronts. The Germans expect the new offensive any day, and say it is the calm before the storm.

More statistics have been published: civilian dwellings in Rome destroyed or very seriously damaged by air raids amount to 2,437.

Friday April 21st

Today is the "birthday of Rome," the day on which the city is supposed to have been founded by Romulus, 753 B.C. In the heyday of Fascism large-scale celebrations were held, but today they have soft-pedalled "manifestations of public enthusiasm" and are not attempting anything beyond a few speeches. Italian

[163]

correspondents at the front speak of heavy reinforcements being brought up by the Allies, both at Cassino and Anzio.

We heard a girl in a tram today sobbing out the story of her father and her two brothers, who were arrested by the Germans for forced labour while they were engaged in their own regular work in a printing establishment. "They told us that those who had regular work would be left in peace," she lamented. She is all alone now, and has no idea where her men folk are.

The parish priest of Lanuvio said Mass at St. John Lateran yesterday for those of his flock who had fled to Rome. They never tire of telling us about his heroism; how he alone remained in the village, combining the functions of pastor, mayor, chemist, doctor and agricultural expert.

Saturday April 22nd

Beppino went on his bicycle into the country yesterday to try to find some food for his family; he went all the way to Fara Sabina but found that, even in that remote place, the peasants will not sell flour for money: they want salt and shoes in exchange. In fact money has very little buying power at present. Regarding prices in general the following table is illuminating:

	1934 (May)	1944 (May)
Bread per kg.	0.56 Lire	120 Lire
Pasta	2.20	200
Meat	7.00	260
Cheese	8.00	500
Shoes (men)	25.00	2000
Hire of room p. day	10.00	100

Though not exhaustive, this gives some idea of the economic situation here.

Sunday April 23rd

The Pope's Villa at Castel Gandolfo has been bombed again; can it be German planes? Or Fascist?

We had several alarms this morning and heard heavy explosions; it seems that the Allied Air Force caught a large German column on the Via Appia and that their petrol lorries blew up.

Prelates who are received in audience by the Pope now bring gifts heretofore unknown. This morning the Bishop of Osimo presented His Holiness with 24,000 kilogrammes of provisions for the city.

Monday April 24th

Private directions issued from the Ministry of Popular Culture to the press at present include the following: "When dealing with the battle for Sebastopol, do not use the expression 'fortress' in speaking of the town, because its fortifications were destroyed by the Germans during the attacks they made for its conquest."

Again: "Do not refer to our brave allies as *'Tedeschi'* but as *'Germanici'*."

Regarding some unfortunate photographs of Mussolini which had appeared: "No photographs of Il Duce are to be published without express authorization from this Ministry." There is a blank in this morning's *Messaggero*. Was it one of those inopportune photographs?

Tuesday April 25th

Rumours of strikes to take place on the first of May are persistent, but it is quite possible that they are only German propaganda, meant to frighten the public and arouse "anticommunist" feeling. Anyone who is opposed to the Nazifascist regime at present is called a "communist," and they are getting every ounce of value out of the bolshevik bogey; when they have nothing else to say, and the military situation is discouraging for the Germans, they start in on bolshevism.

Wednesday April 26th

News of a meeting between Hitler and Mussolini on the 22nd and 23rd of this month has just been released. As usual on these occasions "The political, military and economic conditions of Italy and Germany were discussed in detail," and "Il Duce expressed the determination of the Fascist Republican Government, as sole representative of Italy, to intensify its war effort as one of the Tripartite Powers." The usual chorus of Plenipotentiaries, Ambassadors, Marshals and Under-Secretaries "took part in the discussions." One wonders what they really said, besides the obvious statement: "the game is up."

Three thousand boxes of matches intended for the black market have been sequestrated with a flourish. Yes, we have come to that.

The beggars are going beyond all limits. At first one was sorry for them, but now they are becoming almost rebellious. Today one of them insisted on our giving her more than we had given, and when we refused put her finger on the electric button of our doorbell and kept it there. The whole household rushed to the spot. Was no one answering it? The noise was unbearable! What had happened? And still she went on ringing. We were helpless, unless we were to carry her bodily into the street. We said we would call the police. "I'll slap him if he comes," was the answer. The incident was troublesome, but it had a funny side to it.

Thursday April 27th
It is generally understood that the Fascists put a stop to the plan of having Rome policed by an international force under the Pope's authority. We also hear that "something big" will probably happen this week, i.e., before Wednesday, May 3rd. Beyond that, all is quiet here today and going on as usual: the weather is perfect, the bees are overeating themselves among the wistaria blossoms in our garden, and bombs are falling rhythmically in the distance. Every night caravans of lorries leave the C.I.T. offices in Piazza Esedra, loaded with people bound for the mysterious "north of Italy." A lorry carrying petrol accompanies the caravan, which otherwise would not find enough on the way.

Friday April 28th
The bees may have been having their breakfast among the flowers yesterday, but the people, having less and less to eat for breakfast, dinner and supper, staged bread riots in the Testaccio

quarter as well as near Piazza Fiume quite close to us. The cry was raised: "The brutes are starving us!"—meaning, of course, the Germans. Several bakeries were broken into and looted.

The *Tribuna* this evening publishes a long article on the pontifical food ships, giving their exact number, stating that they were hired in Genoa, that they are small coasting vessels, and that they would probably be able to navigate the Tiber for a certain distance. It even gives the names of two of the ships. What it omits, however, is the fact that, as they did some time ago, the Germans refuse to let them through unless they themselves take 70 per cent of the cargo.

Saturday April 29th

Everyone is beginning to say that the invasion of the Continent will take place in June. That seems to be the most sensible rumour we have heard. My own guess is that it will happen before June 10th, though I have no great faith in anyone's prophetic powers.

N.L. came in today with her sister, who had fled from her country place where S.S. men had threatened to shoot both her and her husband. The reason of the threat was that they had helped British and American prisoners, that an American flag was found concealed in their house, and that some letters, written in English, did not express very complimentary opinions of the Germans. They escaped by miracle, and it will be easier for them to hide in Rome than in the country.

What *would* the Germans say if they searched this house, discovered this diary (which is even less complimentary to them than the last time that fear of its being found crossed my mind) and found the flags, both American and British, which we have put away? They are fine big flags, too.

German women in Rome have had orders to leave the city today; a significant detail, if nothing else. They say that the Gestapo is going also; is it possible?

M.P. tells us that he has seen a contract signed by a big Italian cement company for work on cement fortifications under the direction of the Todt Organization on the La Spezia–Rimini

Line, which must be finished by May 15th. Another sign of withdrawal?

Much publicity is being given to the small amount of extra food which has been allotted to "workers," that is to say, to the men who are working for the Germans or the Fascists. Between May 3rd and May 30th, they will be allowed to buy one small tin of meat, one-fifth of a quart of oil, one pound of sugar and seven ounces of cheese. The headings of these regulations do their best, announcing in heavy type: "Extraordinary distribution of provisions to workers."

Today's confidential instructions to the press bid journalists not to omit articles on General Mazeler completing his first six months as commander of Rome on May 1st. "The German Ambassador has it particularly at heart."

Sure enough, here are the little lyrics congratulating Rome on having been under the command of General Maelzer for twenty-four weeks. They appear, obediently enough, in all the papers. Maelzer, the man who is starving the city, who ordered the execution of the 320 hostages in the Ardeatine Cave, who encourages the black market in order to get a rake-off for himself, the typical Junker; he receives bouquets thrown in such profusion that it is hard to choose the sweetest. Here, however, is one among many:

The sympathetic understanding shown by General Maelzer for all the delicate problems of Rome during his six months in command of the city has thrown into relief his outstanding military and organizing powers to which his brilliant and courageous military career bears witness. To these inborn qualities he adds a lively affection for our country. For this reason his decisions concerning Rome, prompted by a ready intelligence, have made General Maelzer, our comrade and our ally, an outstanding figure in the city and one who is surrounded by esteem and affection.

[168]

Nobody could have done more, could they, in obedience to that Minister's orders?

From what we have been hearing on the wireless about the bombing of Berlin, one wonders if there is anything at all left of it by this time.

Tuesday May 2nd

The much-dreaded strikes came to nothing yesterday. Some of the printers at the *Messaggero* building did not go to work, but they were quickly arrested and sent off to forced labour.

Vatican lorries have again been attacked from the air, and damaged seriously. Of course if German army trucks continue to attach themselves to the Vatican columns, bombs must be expected to fall on them.

Wednesday May 3rd

The class of 1914 has also been called up for military service. Hitler's Generals have probably been complaining that Italy is not furnishing enough cannon fodder.

A number of young men belonging to the Catholic Radio Centre have been arrested and taken to Via Tasso, because they were supposed to be carrying on "patriot" activities.

Thursday May 4th

A time bomb was found concealed in the big building in Corso d'Italia where the German offices are. It was removed before it exploded, but the display of armed force on every side of the building is truly impressive. Machine guns are trained on the side streets which lead to Corso d'Italia, and there are sentinels everywhere.

H.W., aged 18, and not accustomed to be held up when she is in a hurry, was on her way to our house a little while ago, and passed a German sentry guarding a roadway that no one was supposed to cross. She started calmly to take a short cut across the road. The sentry shouted: "Halt!" Foolishly she began to

run, when a bullet whistled past her ear. She won't take that
short cut again.

Friday May 5th

The Germans have arrested another priest who was helping
patriots. He had already been caught once and released afterward. This time when he saw he was followed he made for St.
Mary Major's, thinking he would be safe there. On the way in
the policeman who was pursuing him grabbed at him, whereupon
the priest knocked him down, and there was a scuffle during
which the former freed himself and entered the basilica. The
S.S. then entered it, and their officer telephoned to the Vatican
for permission to surround St. Mary Major's and its various exits.
This could not be refused, under the circumstances, and the
arrest was made. The prisoner was taken to Via Tasso.

Saturday May 6th

We are very pleased to learn that the outstanding questions
between the Allies and Spain have been successfully settled.

The Vatican authorities apparently have reason to fear thieves
—or is it Germans? They are doubling the guards in the Vatican
Museums, and are placing some on duty there even at night. You
never know, of course.

The Allied Air Force is working such havoc among the German columns and supply dumps along the roads leading to Rome
that not a day passes without the sound of explosions; furious
paragraphs appear in the press about "brutal attacks on road
traffic." The Fascists seem to have forgotten the days of the Battle
of Britain, when they requested of Hitler "to be allowed the
honour of sharing in the attack on England."

Anyone passing near Piazza di Siena, in the Villa Borghese,
these evenings at about seven o'clock, will see groups of dejected
men and women waiting under the trees near a line of vans,
lorries and motor char-à-bancs. One of us asked a man with a
suitcase if he were going north. "Ask at the office," he answered,
with a jerk of his head in that direction. Some distance away the
same question was asked of a woman: "The policeman will tell

you," she said dully. Were they part of the forced labour service, sworn to secrecy? It was all uncanny and depressing. We were afraid of being shadowed if we asked the question a third time, so we were left guessing.

Sunday May 7th

Every day we expect the invasion. Every day we listen to victory talk on the wireless. Every day we notice growing tension around us, and ill-concealed hopes of the speedy arrival of the Allies. When *will* they come?

Monday May 8th

Food shops now shut at once when they get a message to say that there is a possibility of their being looted. Our grocer did it the other day; not that he has anything particular to sell in the shop, but he feared the place being wrecked.

The curfew is extended for our benefit. It will begin as from today at 9 P.M. and end at 5 A.M.; so, on these soft May evenings Romans may actually stay out until nine o'clock, or eight o'clock "by the sun." We have to be thankful for very small mercies in times like these.

German soldiers and officers are swarming into Rome again; they seem more numerous than ever. No one knows why.

A real event took place today: we each had our monthly ration of 3½ ounces of meat for dinner. It looked and tasted like donkey meat, but it may really have been something better.

Tuesday May 9th

Our cat ate a rat. No, this is not turning into a kindergarten textbook. He was just making history. The point is that he is, like most cats who live in houses (and Heaven help those who live in the streets or among the ruins, as they do in Rome), thoroughly spoiled. He is lordly, lazy and proud. He will only eat a mouse if it is young and tender. In the way of other eatables, what we get, he shares. Today, however, his whole being rose up against a diet of macaroni, dried peas and rice, cooked

[171]

in water with no cheese, no butter, no gravy, no milk. With grim determination he withdrew to the cellar, killed and ate a big rat—all except the tail, which we think he is going to appeal to the cook to make into soup for him. The historical fact that he was underlining is that the food conditions are bad in Rome at present.

Wednesday May 10th

A funeral took place today, with such crowds attending it that they almost blocked the traffic in the neighbourhood of the Campo Verano. It was that of a woman who was shot while standing in a bread queue, and who made what were called "seditious remarks." Poor thing, she was only complaining of hunger, most probably.

Ridiculously small details can be held as seditious today. In a tram two women were talking about their husbands. One said: "Mine is in the Royal Navy." At this a Fascist called out and said: "In the *Royal* Navy?" "Oh, well, does a word matter so much?" asked the woman. "Very much indeed," said the Fascist, and took her name and address and full particulars concerning her. I only hope she gave him false ones.

Thursday May 11th

The lull on the Anzio and Cassino fronts must mean something these days. Of course military secrets have to be kept, but everyone is agreed that something great will happen in a few days.

The patriots are becoming still more active. A Fascist soldier was killed yesterday in a street near Villa Borghese, but the murderer got away. The Germans have offered a large reward for information regarding him.

Friday May 12th

Well, it has begun. It is happening. It seems too good to be true, but there is the wireless report of a powerful Allied offensive against the Gustav Line. If only it does not end, as so many of the other actions undertaken against the Germans during these months have ended, in "patrol activities." One mustn't be pessimistic, but, as I pointed out some time ago, our expectations have inevitably lost some of their elasticity.

Saturday May 13th

Considering that the British radio broadcast the news every ten minutes yesterday of the great offensive having begun, I think that one may safely believe it. The Italian press and radio are very quiet about it.

Sunday May 14th

The offensive has put new life into us, and new hope into the Italians. The Allies are "progressing slowly," but as long as they do progress, all is well.

The Fascists are starting a private collection to pay for weapons for their army. The appeal has a pathetic sound about it. They have nothing, no arms, no clothes, no boots, no supplies.

Monday May 15th

News of our progress against the Gustav Line continues.

In all the Roman churches people are praying for peace with renewed hope. They know that the first step toward it will be the defeat of the Germans. The transfer of the 8th Army from the east to the west of Italy was a gigantic achievement to have accomplished with such speed and secrecy.

Tuesday May 16th

The papers publish a photograph of Marshal Graziani in conversation with a recruit to the Republican army. He looks old, haggard, and worn. No wonder. He has soldierlike qualities, and must realize that defeat cannot be far off. The press is beginning to refer to "elastic defence," meaning that the Germans are on the run.

Late news says that we have made a breach in the Gustav Line.

[173]

Wednesday May 17th

Our progress continues to be satisfactory, says the B.B.C.; heights have been taken and a bridge-head established across the Rapido.

News in the Italian papers informs us that Graziani has been to the front; and tram fares in Rome have been doubled. Also that the Russians have been "driven back by the Germans."

Thursday May 18th

Better and better: we have broken the Gustav Line.

Confidential instructions to the press today direct "front line correspondents not to speak of the existence of a line of defence named after Adolf Hitler."

There is a terrible scarcity of paper at present, but a brave new periodical is coming out called *"Roma Repubblicana."* It is calculated to help "morale."

Friday May 19th

Wonderful news of Allied successes against the Hitler Line.

"Manoeuvred defence" is praised in the Fascist papers as a splendid military achievement.

People in Rome can talk of nothing else than the offensive, and are already settling dates for the arrival of the Allies—as they have so often done in the past.

Saturday May 20th

Cassino is taken!

Sunday May 21st

According to the B.B.C. "we are sweeping victoriously on."

Gaeta is extraordinarily important—and we have taken it. All other news items or impressions seem insignificant beside what we are hearing about the offensive.

This morning we went to the solemn Requiem in St. Peter's for the late Cardinal O'Connell, Archbishop of Boston. The right transept was draped in black and gold, and provided a fine setting for the catafalque and the altar. Perosi himself conducted the Papal choir, which executed some of his own compositions. Harold Tittmann, diplomatic Chargé d'Affaires of the United States, received the Cardinals' condolences at the end of the ceremony. All the English-speaking people in Rome appeared to be present, everyone knew everyone else. Was it perhaps a remote prelude to victory, this coming together of citizens of the United Nations?

On the way out of the basilica we stopped by the little Chapel of the Relics, inside whose sealed door lay the incorrupt remains of Pope Pius X, deceased thirty years ago, and whose body had been disinterred for examination as part of the Process of Canonization. They will be buried again shortly "in forma privatissima." Odd little bunches of flowers had been fastened to the bronze work of the chapel door, just as they used to be laid on his tomb in the crypt.

When we neared the vestibule we were joined by three British prisoners of war who had taken refuge in the Vatican City. They wanted to talk English to someone, they said. Two of them were naval men who escaped from their prison camp disguised in Italian uniforms, and made their way to St. Peter's. A pontifical policeman who tried to put them out got a vigorous punch in the jaw—whereupon he summoned other policemen to help him, and our two were being carried out bodily, when the Secretary of the British Legation to the Holy See arrived and took them under his protection. One of the onlookers, with great presence of mind, had rushed off to tell him what was happening, and he got there in time. The third was the famous aviator of whom we had all heard, who, after bailing out, climbed over the wall of the Vatican City and reported to the British Minister. We had a few moments' talk—so much to say, and so little time to say it in—but as soon as the British are here the three are coming around to see us. In the meantime they are safe, unless of course, the Germans raid the Vatican City. I cannot bring myself to think that they will do it.

People who greeted us were in high spirits and making guesses as to exactly what day the Allies would reach Rome. With Fondi, Terracina and Pico in our hands, there is good reason for hope. Only one man croaked: "The Germans have brought down large reinforcements to meet the Allies, I hear them passing our place at night—we're going to have trouble." I wonder. Have they enough reserves? A Cassandra who resides in the Vatican City prophesied doom and devastation; the Germans would inevitably enter, take off the hundreds of people who were in hiding there, and make a clean sweep of all the others. Well, they haven't done it yet, and we can only live from day to day, now.

The enemy obviously realizes that he is on the point of being beaten, and is showing signs of it here. Within the last few days they have renewed the intensive search for Jews; S.S. men arrived at the house of a Swedish Jewess, married to an Italian, and said: "Tomorrow we shall come for you." The Swedish Minister could do nothing. Another, merely of Jewish descent, came to us this afternoon begging to be told where to hide; happily we were able to find a place for her. In the course of these months of German occupation, persecution of Jews followed a course parallel to the persecution in Germany. Brutally rounded up without warning, men, women and children were deported wholesale, many of them to unknown destinations, such as Poland; numbers were killed outright, and others were left to starve. The following few statistics are trustworthy. Of the 10,000 Jews who remained in Rome after the Fascist "Racial Laws" were passed, about 6,000 were victims of Nazi brutality. Among these, roughly 1,000 are known to have been killed, that is, either executed or left to die of hunger and want. Of the remaining 5,000 there is no trace at present. How many of these will return when the war is over? It is a terrible question to ask, for the answer may be a terrible one. But more terrible still is the responsibility weighing on the authors and instigators of this appalling "race war." No one will ever know, except a few Vatican authorities, how many Jews enjoyed the personal protection of the Pope in their darkest days. Food, lodging, clothing and occupation were found for them in the Vatican itself, by special directions of the Sovereign Pontiff. Warm and generous sympathy went out to them from Catholics throughout the city, regardless of race or creed, often at great personal risk.

Via Tasso is not enough for the Nazi spies, and they have opened another torture house for extracting information from patriots. It is managed by their satellites, the Italian "S.S." men. It was known as Pensione Jaccarino before they took it over, and has retained its name. They have plain-clothes detectives strolling about near the entrance, and if any passers-by look up at the window, or stop to listen to strange sounds, they are arrested and taken inside, as possible accomplices. The Nazifascists' one idea is to catch all patriots and put them to death; they have failed to find most of the Roman ones, so their best chance is to torture the few they have in order to get evidence against others. This new place in Via Romagna is fitted up with the same hideous instruments as the one in Via Tasso; pincers for pulling out teeth and fingernails, whips, rods, and means of heating knives red hot. Some of our friends who live near there and hear the screams and groans, particularly at night, say that it is diabolical. One of them has received word that no one in his flat, which is close to Pensione Jaccarino, must go up on the roof terrace of the house, and that the shutters must always be kept closed. The S.S. are so very frightened of a stray shot coming their way! It seems impossible to be writing all this in cold blood, as if it were just a matter of course, but then it *is* a matter of course; it would be incredible if we were not right up against it. And one is so utterly helpless! There is no rescue possible for those unfortunate patriots. Hanging will be but a poor punishment for their torturers when the day of reckoning comes at last.

Four more refugees have arrived, begging to be sheltered. We can't refuse. I wonder where and how they will shake down. Poor frightened things. They were forcibly evacuated from Lanuvio by armed Germans and locked up in a big building on the outskirts of Rome, preparatory to being transferred to a concentration camp in the country. They managed to escape from their prison, where they were guarded by Fascists with guns and whips. They are horrified, not only at the cruelty but that any Italian should behave so. They expect it from the Germans, but not from their own.

We hear that Kesselring has called up all his available reserves, both from the Adriatic sector and from Nettuno, to try to hold us back on the coast and in the Liri Valley. So the man who said it, at St. Peter's yesterday, was right after all. Yet I don't think that they can really hold up our offensive. Rome is tense. The Romans are in high spirits, but they dread what the Germans may do before they go. Rome Radio (Fascist-controlled) has warned the inhabitants to store up all the water they can, meaning that the mains will probably be dynamited, as well as the electric plant. The panic that is beginning to show itself recalls the panic last September when Rome was occupied. Anxiety to conceal young men who are wanted by the Fascists for the army or for forced labour, and desire to protect their families, in case of reprisals, is increased by the knowledge that tomorrow at midnight the time "graciously granted by Il Duce to defaulters from military service" expires. For weeks press and radio have never ceased to advise, order, coax, beg, encourage and direct defaulters to come and be forgiven, to join the ranks of the Republican army, assuring them that they would suffer no penalty for delay—until midnight on May 25th. After that they would be searched out, arrested and shot in the back as deserters.

Yesterday, perhaps to show that they were in earnest, the Germans held a man-hunt in Via Nazionale, cutting off a certain portion of it, and rounding up all the men within the area. All this adds to the tension here.

Peasants coming in from the Castelli say that there are placards in Frascati forbidding any food except green vegetables to be taken to Rome. They tell us that the Fascists want to starve Rome deliberately, because there has been so little response on the part of the Romans to their appeal to join them, as also great reluctance to follow the "Republican Government" to the northern provinces; they are continually representing those places as centres of peace and plenty, where food is cheap and pay is high. Refugees crowd in to Rome, and we are approaching starvation point more rapidly every day; the Nazifascists encourage the black market and get a handsome profit on the side; yet no one joins their army, and no one goes north. Their only recruits consist of weedy boys who would do anything for an extra fifty lire or so, and who strut about in black shirts carrying rifles and revolvers. P. was looking at one of them the other day, fascinated by his stupid face and arrogant pose; the youth approached him with rifle cocked: "Look at me like that," he threatened, "and I'll shoot you. I'm armed." P. turned his back and strolled off.

Speaking of black market goods: at present rice costs $175 a sack, if you can find it, and can afford it; butter is $4 a pound, and oil $10 a quart—again if you have the money, which you probably haven't.

Guidonia, the famous secret "air city" near Tivoli, apple of Mussolini's eye and boast of the Fascist regime, whence Balbo and his men set out for their transatlantic flight to Chicago— Guidonia today is nothing but a heap of rubble. The Germans spent a whole morning blowing it up, with its storehouses, repair shops and airfields. And that is another significant event.

Wednesday May 24th

A perfectly new Allied offensive has been launched against the German positions south of Anzio. It ought to end in a regular break-through, and one can foresee the junction of the two armies. It comes as a complete surprise to the Germans.

The B.B.C. is now broadcasting official instructions to members of the Underground Front in Europe. They are very detailed, and among the psychological information which we can furnish for the Allies are descriptions of the expressions of German officers. Now that is a little difficult for us, here. Every important one who goes by has exactly the same kind of expression. It must be taught in their military colleges, and is a strange combination of fierce determination and complete mistrust. It is not a pleasing sight.

Word has gone round that Parioli, the high, new, fashionable quarter, is to be evacuated because the Germans will pass through it when they retreat. They do not want to be fired at from windows as when they left Naples. There is also a rumour that the same will happen to those who live in Via Salaria and Via Flaminia, so masses of people are again looking for temporary lodgings. Really, what with refugees from outside the city, and people hiding from the Germans, and now this set wanting to change their residences, life is becoming altogether too complicated. And there is still that undercurrent of panic.

Thursday May 25th

Explosions and the sound of artillery reach us fitfully by night and by day at present.

Events small and great are bringing with them a steady crescendo of activities for us, as well as a crescendo of mixed feelings. Late yesterday evening more refugees came, having escaped from that concentration camp, like the others. Then this morning, still more, fleeing from the renewed bombing at Frascati—men, women and children. Our total is at present 36. One gets to know the refugee face so well, they are all alike: drawn and anxious, with a strange dingy pallor. They are touchingly grateful to be housed and fed. Among them are six young men of military age. What if the Germans raid us? Our peasant guests have brought two horses of theirs to save them from the Germans, "Picchietto" and "Biscotto"; they are tethered in a shady corner of the garden. All these refugees have a special claim on us, so it is not like receiving complete strangers; they are mainly relatives of maids we had before the war.

Later came news of the Allies' spectacular successes in the Liri Valley, of our tanks thundering through the Adolf Hitler Line, and of the junction of our forces from Anzio with those coming northward from Gaeta. People dropped in, bubbling over with optimism, and wanting to know from us exactly when the Allies would reach Rome. A tale was current that the Allies had thrown down leaflets directing Romans to get in supplies for five days. We did not meet anyone who had seen them; and even if they had, where could one get extra provisions? We are hardly able to get enough for one day at a time.

The Germans have just blown up the Ciampino airfield. Wild conjectures are being made as to what they can and will do when they withdraw. Then, apprehension is increasing as to what will take place after midnight tonight, when the time expires for men of military age to report themselves. Fascist agents have busily spread rumours that every house in Rome will be systematically searched for these young men, as well as for older anti-Fascists and Jews.

What can one possibly say to comfort panic-stricken relatives of the hidden men? "I'm certain they will be all right" sounds feeble enough, but if said with conviction it seems to reassure them somewhat.

And all the time the Allies are nearing Rome: joy at their approach is balanced by dread of German savagery. By evening it was said that the Allies had taken Albano, Velletri and Lanuvio, but the report is not confirmed.

As I write it is getting on for midnight, and the streets are strangely quiet; there is no sound but "halt!" occasionally shouted at a passing vehicle, followed by the screech of brakes. A German plane is flying low over the city.

This evening the *Osservatore Romano* fearlessly published a protest against this threatened shooting of patriots and others in hiding. In brief, it ran as follows:

Tonight the time fixed for all those who have military obligations expires. From articles in the press and from rumours that have been spread, we are led to fear a renewal of civil strife. Patience will give way to violence, and a fresh stage on the road to Calvary will open for our tormented country.

Everything is said and done today in the name of Italy, of her prestige, of her defence, of her destiny. But we believe that all these things are never in such peril as when they are defended by means of civil war, and we are convinced that never was civil war more fatal both morally and politically than the one which is now raging here, in presence of armed foreigners encamped on our soil.

During the present world war immense burdens have accumulated on the consciences of individuals and of groups, but, at least, let not this further responsibility be added to them, at this particular juncture and in the midst of grief, destruction, of mass exodus, of poverty and of hunger; at this time, when we should put aside wrongs and rancour, as well as temptations to revenge, and be moved only by the strong impetus of charity to help each other in the name of pity and of peace.

God forgives much in return for kindness to our fellow-men. Let today's kindness, in this most painful situation of our country, be the cessation of that violence which arouses answering violence. Let us not do unto others that which we would not have done unto us. This, let it be remembered, is the condition of God's pardon; it is the only good omen for that of men.

Headings in the Fascist papers read: "After midnight punishment will be relentless." And as if to exemplify their relentless character, Fascist courts have already passed sentence of death on the four admirals whose trial began some weeks ago. Today two of them were executed as traitors: Admiral Campioni, who commanded the Italian forces in the Aegean and who loyally accepted the armistice, and Admiral Mascherpa, who was at Leros, acting under the former, and who also obeyed Badoglio's orders. Admiral Priamo and Admiral Pavesi, who commanded respectively in Sicily and Pantelleria, were condemned in their absence. There is something particularly revolting in these judicial murders; the Republicans, like rats in a corner, are as savage as the Germans, if not more so, for their days are evil and their time is short.

Midnight. Nothing is happening—in this neighbourhood, at any rate. Not a creature is stirring. No one has been knocked up. There is a queer silence over everything, like the silence of death.

Friday May 26th

We were out early this morning for Mass at Sant'Ignazio. The streets were deserted, and Rome seemed paralyzed. In one part of Via del Tritone a queue had gathered, mainly of women. They were very noisy, and looked angry. There was not a single German to be seen either when we went or when we returned, except one in a car, who seemed in a great hurry. Is it possible that they have left in the night? We saw one man, obviously in disguise, probably an Italian patriot. He was dressed as a Dominican; nearly everything about him was correct, except his cloak which was much too short, and he wore the hood pulled down over his face. Dominicans in Rome wear hats, not hoods. A woman who was passing turned to look at him curiously.

There is news of heavy fighting in and around Cisterna, where we are advancing from house to house, it seems. Our refugees who are swarming all over the place by now, and are thoroughly at home, tell us that the Allies are at Albano—but that can't be true. At 2 o'clock this morning there was a terrific explosion which woke the whole of Rome. The Germans were probably blowing up some building, or perhaps one of their own ammunition dumps. Allied bombers hit an aqueduct somewhere near here yesterday, and the water is cut off in this neighbourhood.

We have been hearing bombs, ack-ack guns, heavy shells and unidentified explosions all day. It is strange how accustomed one grows to these sounds, and, after all, the only thing to do is to carry on with one's customary occupations. Poor Tivoli, where the Germans had large stores of ammunition, was terribly knocked about this morning in an air raid; 1,000 civilians were killed and half the population was wounded. A great deal of damage was done to houses and churches, and they say that the Villa d'Este was struck also. Rocca di Papa was shelled from the sea, and Frascati was bombed once more.

We have housed a few more refugees since this morning, and our total has now reached forty-one. I think we shall have to stop at that number. Some we cook for, and some do their own cooking. As a result there is a charcoal stove going in the tool-house, and another primitive fireplace made of bricks up on our terrace among the nasturtiums and oleanders.

We have advised the young men of military age who are among them, in case the house should be searched, to jump over the wall which separates us from the garden next door, and, without saying anything to the porter, to hide behind some automobiles (also concealed) back of a conservatory.

The local papers lashed themselves into a fury over yesterday's article in the *Osservatore Romano*. Bruno Spampanato, the truculent editor of the *Messaggero*, simply called the writer of the article all the names he could think of for the space of two columns; it was like an angry child making faces at an adversary, and about as conclusive. He tried to be very, very impudent and bold. This valiant Bruno now sleeps at the Hotel Flora, where the Germans will protect him from the patriots if necessary; he is afraid to go home, yet he is so brave on paper. Poor Bruno.

The Anzio wireless has begun giving information about spies and informers who are working for the Germans. It broadcasts their names, addresses and personal characteristics. Listeners-in are delighted, and it is the regular thing to come to the radio

[183]

armed with pencil and paper, so as to have your own list of spies. The individuals are furious, but what can they do about it? The patriots of the Underground Front in Rome are so much cleverer than the Nazifascists, that their information is accurate to an uncanny degree.

Saturday May 27th

Two of the informers mentioned yesterday by the Anzio wireless are the porter of a house which we know, and his wife. They have specialized in reporting the whereabouts of Jews. This morning they are sitting in their lodge shedding tears; and well they may.

Hope rises as the Allies progress. We have waited for over eight months, but now every added hour seems interminable. They are at Velletri today, but it looks as if they would not come straight to Rome, preferring to cut the Via Casilina at Valmontone, as they have already cut the Via Appia. In that case perhaps the Germans will retreat eastwards, and not through Rome. G.C., who is at the Grand Hotel, says that a German diplomat who is staying there has begun to do his packing. Fascist journalists and officials are leaving in numbers, prudently, while the going is good.

Yesterday the Germans blew up the Littorio airfield, and the neighbouring bridge over the Tiber. The former is an excellent one, and used to be the civilian airport of Rome; it is about two kilometres out on Via Salaria.

The threatened search for patriots, from house to house, is not taking place, after all. And for an excellent reason. No one would undertake it. The job was declined in turn by the P.A.I. Italian police who had served in Africa and who have been working with and for the Germans (though a number of them are patriots); by the plain-clothes police belonging to the Questura, Caruso's men; by the Metropolitan City traffic-police, who have carried rifles of late; by the blackshirt S.S., and finally by the Germans themselves. And they all refused for the same reason. An old and obvious human reason. They were afraid. Popular feeling is running high, the patriots are armed and have plenty of ammunition, and a popular rising might easily follow police action of that sort. No one wanted to put a match to that particular powder barrel, above all with the Allies thundering, as it were, at the gates of the city. So the terrible threat formulated for "after midnight on May 25th" has come to nothing, like so many other Fascist undertakings.

Sunday May 28th (Whitsunday)

The Allies' progress is eminently satisfactory, though we are still bracing ourselves for the horrors of retreating German hordes. Kesselring has brought down more reinforcements and is trying to hold Valmontone at all costs, so as to give his 80,000 men from the Cassino front time to withdraw. The renowned Hermann Goering Division is in action, and is giving the Allies less trouble than most; it has been filled up with boys of 17 and 18 to replace earlier losses.

Last night there was a steady stream of German tanks, guns and lorries passing through the city northward bound. The cannonade from the Castelli goes on as constantly as ever, and report says that the Allies are at Lanuvio. Planes flew over during the night, probably carrying German officers getting out of tight corners.

One of our refugees, who walked to the Castelli to see how things were going, reported a delightful conversation overheard between a German soldier and a Blackshirt, speculating as to what would happen when the Allies arrived. "Me," said Jerry, "I do this"—and he held up his hands; "you," pointing an imaginary gun at the Republican's chest, "poum, poum, finish!" Our Frascati refugees say that the Germans are leaving there, taking their wounded with them. The state of these latter can better be imagined than described. The boys said that blood was dripping from the floor of the ambulances. Large numbers of Italian wounded have come into Rome from the Anzio sector, where the much advertised Barbarigo Battalion was placed in the front line by its German masters. From the propaganda photographs in the press and on posters, it seemed to be composed of little boys of 16 and 17.

It is pleasantly warm, and spring is at its height; this is proved by the pretty green grass growing in the streets which are paved with stone blocks; there is next to no motor traffic except that of the Germans, and they always take the asphalted streets. Somehow "grass growing in the streets of Rome" has a fourteenth-century sound about it.

On account of damage to the aqueducts, emergency pipes have been rigged up at intervals in the streets, and the people go to get their own water from them in pails and bottles. The queues that gather are of a very different temper from those of last March. Then they were mournful, dispirited, almost without hope or energy; now a cheerful buzz emanates from them, in fact the drawing of water becomes almost a social occasion. The leitmotif of the buzz is: "The Germans are on the run—it won't be long before the Allies are here!" Our refugees show their appreciation of our hospitality by carrying water for us, keeping all our tubs filled. Among them Michele, who insists on taking a twenty-minute walk twice a day to get what he considers to be really good drinking water for us from Via dei Lucchesi. He goes off with three *fiaschi* in a black oilskin bag and returns with the regularity of a clock. Water, by the way, is heavy.

Cesare, another of our refugees, has to start early tomorrow morning to get more fodder for the horses. It is dangerous for him, but the grass in our garden, which we offered him, would only last them a day or so. The curfew ends at 5 o'clock, so he will start then.

Monday May 29th

Cesare got back safely at about 8.30 though outside Rome, near the new Cinema City, three German lorries approached his cart, and he had a narrow escape from the machine guns of Allied planes which power-dived and destroyed the lorries. Our planes don't miss much on the roads at present. Cesare took cover in a ditch, and came to no harm. The horses, Picchietto and Biscotto, seem pleased with the fresh hay he brought them.

As the Germans have taken all the machinery from the Roman broadcasting station, Radio Roma will be heard no more for the present. Obviously, they don't want patriots or the Allies to be able to issue directions conveniently. If only they don't confiscate our own radios! That would be a real tragedy. The B.B.C. tells us this morning that the Allies are advancing all along the line, and are only twenty kilometres from Rome. If they get here soon, then the harvest can be saved. The wheat is magnificent this year, but it must be harvested not later than June 10th. Until then it will be a little too green to be burnt by the Germans.

Partly for propaganda, partly to prevent food riots, and partly because the people are starving, General Maelzer, commander of Rome, has ordered rice, flour and bread to be distributed free in the poorer parts of the city, where the people are in an ugly mood. For instance, no German dares to go alone in the Trastevere. That district, the Garbatella and the Testaccio were the ones chosen. The lorry carrying the food was accompanied by a crowd of Italian and German journalists and camera men, and the papers published columns of praise of General Maelzer's generosity. They did not mention the fact that he is one of the "black market kings" into whose pockets pass large sums gained in illicit traffic in food and tobacco.

The sounds of war continue to echo around us day and night, but unusually continuous pounding of guns in the Alban Hills began to be heard about midday.

The electric current for such buses and trams as remain to us was cut off this morning, so one has to walk or not go at all. It is really better for everyone to stay indoors, especially men. Leone, one of our men from Lanuvio, was arrested in the street today and taken off to the police station to be enrolled in the forced labour service.—It seems that Mussolini has promised Hitler one million five hundred thousand labourers.—They told Leone that tomorrow he would be taken to the barracks where Nello was in March, and then given further orders. Happily, someone from the Vatican called here this afternoon, and promised to arrange for Leone to be freed. These individual arrests are certainly disquieting. M.'s porter, a quiet, harmless man, was arrested recently by the Fascists, for no apparent reason, taken to the German torture house in Via Tasso, and was kept there for four days and nights in a dark cell, without food. After that he was suddenly released, without explanation. His hair turned quite white while he was there.

The Hotel de la Ville in Via Sistina (called "Brighter Berlin"), which was the GHQ for German transport, is empty today; but in spite of that the tempo of life seems a little slower. The wireless assures us that the Allies are making progress, but we were hoping for something short, sharp and decisive, perhaps even spectacular. Kesselring is hanging on at Valmontone, and the Allies have not cut the Casilina at that point, yet. We have secured a number of strong positions, but not those that will be decisive for Rome. Oh, well!

Some time ago the Germans forbade the use of bicycles within the city limits, but permitted tricycles for the delivery of goods. Today a peremptory order is issued to the effect that: "The Commander of the Police of the Open City of Rome [the little farce of the Open City is still kept up industriously] decrees that it is forbidden to ride bicycles camouflaged as tricycles or having motorettes or electric batteries attached to them." Ingenious little third wheels had been added to many bicycles after the fashion of trailers. The Germans are apparently fearful of other cyclist murders.

Orders have been issued to proprietors of houses and gardens to report wells, artesian or otherwise, which may exist on their property. The authorities are getting ready for a serious water shortage. I hope we shan't be reduced to using the Tiber water. Are the Germans really going to wreck all the mains? That is the question we ask ourselves all day and every day.

The Vatican has tightened up facilities for admission within its precincts. Even to enter St. Peter's, various documents have to be shown. One gets accustomed to carring a sort of dossier about; a mere identity card is not sufficient.

This evening's *Osservatore Romano* protests against last Tuesday's bombing of the Benedictine Monastery of Santa Scolastica at Subiaco. The great Renaissance cloister was destroyed, the rest of the monastery was rendered uninhabitable, and a student and a workman were killed. It resembles Monte Cassino on a smaller scale, and the kindest thing one can say is that the bombing must have been done by mistake. Unlike Monte Cassino, it was not even a useful observation post. There were no German supply dumps near it, and it had been used as a hospital since last April. It is completely isolated, on the slopes above the Aniene River, and is older even than Monte Cassino, having been one of St. Benedict's first foundations.

The Battle of the Castelli is raging out in the hills, and German heavy artillery is pounding our approaches to Rome—but not preventing our advance, on the whole. We have taken Arce in the Liri Valley, but not Valmontone as yet.

They say that the Germans in the city have held an evacuation rehearsal, and that they can withdraw inside of one hour. Excellent, if it is true. We are anxiously waiting for that hour to strike.

Leone has returned from his prison barracks, and the welcome he got from the rest of our peasant colony was impressive; from the noise they made, someone said they thought the Allies had arrived. We asked him if he had slept at all. He said, "No, I stood all night, the floor was so dirty."

Everyone says that all the public services *have* been mined. This evening's papers carry cheery paragraphs reassuring the citizens of Rome, telling them not to be anxious about the water supply, because, should it be necessary, the authorities are prepared to utilize existing machinery for filtering the water of the Tiber. But, is the machinery there? No. Can the Tiber be filtered? Doubtful. Could anyone drink it? No.

The steady thud of artillery stopped at midday. Have we knocked them out? At 7.30 A.M. we heard the screech of a power dive repeated several times, and the rattle of machine guns, quite near. A German officer told E.G. that, when the Allies finally broke through at Valmontone, they had orders to make straight for Genoa as best they could; individually, if necessary. The enemy is keeping up appearances in the city, at any rate, though numbers of them have left. All the luggage of the officers at the big hotels in Via Veneto was taken off yesterday, but sentinels still stand at the doors, and policemen prevent pedestrians from passing on the pavement next to the hotels.

A fresh rumour—optimistic, this time—says insistently that the Pope has promised the Germans that, if they do no damage to the city as they withdraw, he will make himself responsible for all their wounded whom they might leave behind; reports as to the number of the wounded vary between 20,000 and 40,000.

This morning the Republican (i.e. Fascist, i.e. Blackshirt, i.e. neo-Fascist or Nazifascist—different names for the same thing) Government shot Alberto Coppola, head of the Pharmacy Supply Organization. He was found guilty of having sold at black market prices thirty-five sacks of sugar, entrusted to him for distribution to chemists for making up prescriptions. For once they appear to have acted justly; but was Coppola really the guilty one? The greatest black-market profiteers are the Germans. General Maelzer, in command of the city, and who likes to be thought of as "King of Rome," has wonderful devices for making money twice over. He will accumulate, for example, a large store of tobacco which his agent will dispose of at a high price to minor Italian black-market dealers. A few days later, the German S.S. are sent to raid the latter and confiscate their stocks, because they are "held illegally"; so they return to good General Maelzer.

We are immensely cheered by the news, broadcast from Anzio, that the Allies are bringing to Rome foodstuffs of every kind, except oil and flour. If they bring tinned lard, we can do without oil; and, after all, we have had so little bread and "pasta" of late, we can wait a few weeks more for flour, particularly if there are other things to supplement them.

The Pope has been trying to arrange for food ships to come to Rome from Spain and Portugal, and the provisions he has purchased are ready at the ports; but, according to the Roman press, "final formalities have yet to be concluded." One of those "formalities" is the German refusal to let the ships come up the Tiber, unless they themselves are given 70 per cent of the cargo. Of course, the Holy Father cannot agree to such terms, anxious as he is to feed the starving city. That condition, obviously, does not appear in the press, but everyone knows about it.

Lack of food has had an alarmingly slimming effect on everyone in Rome, not only on the poor, but on the man-in-the-street and on one's friends. It gives one a heartache to see it. No longer is it complimentary to allude to loss of weight; on the contrary, the subject is tactfully avoided.

The Allies have taken Frosinone and Sora, both of them important places, but the line from Valmontone to the sea is still unbroken. A B.B.C. commentator says breezily "Rome, of course, is a prize, but how much better for General Alexander to surround Kesselring and settle his hash before entering the city." Oh yes? Is it? We are not strategists, armchair or otherwise, but we have practical knowledge of the urgent need of liberating Rome. In spite of the above comment, and of the fact that Valmontone still holds out, everyone here talks as if it were only a matter of days or even hours before the Fifth Army arrives.

I have just had a request from an Italian for the words of "Tipperary"; as they put it in commercial letters, "I shall comply with pleasure."

There is a strange little paragraph in this evening's papers to the effect that yesterday evening a chimney fire took place at 38 Via Romagna, in a house owned by Signor Carlo Jaccarino, and that a good deal of damage was done to the building. That, of course, is the famous Pensione Jaccarino, the torture house used by the Italian S.S. battalion. Jaccarino himself was denounced two evenings ago by Radio Anzio, in its list of spies and informers. Do they want an excuse for leaving the place? Are the rats deserting the sinking ship? The S.S. are distinctly nervous. Anything more alien to the Italian character than an S.S. organization can hardly be imagined, and yet some of them have copied their German masters even in that. And the Germans despise them utterly. The leader of the Fascist group belonging to the Ostiense district was murdered yesterday.

Guns booming nearer than ever, day and night. The Allies have taken Velletri, Lariano, Férentino, Veroli and Sgurgola, but not Valmontone, the big key position. We must be patient.

This morning the Pope received the Cardinals, who presented their good wishes in honour of his name day. The Sacred College is much diminished in numbers, and it is expected that soon after the war is over, he will hold a Consistory for the appointment of many new ones. It was arranged that his reply to the

Cardinals should be broadcast. He spoke of his hopes of a lasting peace, based on Christian principles, of mercy to the vanquished, of his anxiety that the city of Rome should be spared the horrors of war, and of his efforts to provide food for the Romans. He also pointed out that Rome had received more refugees than any other city in Italy.

The Pope's concluding remarks about the numbers of refugees in Rome are borne out by statistics. Last summer the population of Rome amounted to 1,500,000; at present it is 2,000,000. No wonder there is a food shortage; apart from what the Germans have done toward starving the city.

It is said that last night the Pope sent for the German Ambassador, and kept him from 11 P.M. until 1 A.M., talking about the possibilities of not defending Rome, once the Allies had broken through their line in the Castelli, and of not destroying the city as they withdrew. It is understood that the Pope was in a large measure successful.

The Fascist Ministry which controls the press issues confidential directions to the editors from time to time. My source of information is also confidential, but absolutely reliable. Yesterday instructions were sent out as follows: "Journalists are requested to write at length on the forthcoming musical season, which is opening with the Comic Opera Company at the Quirino Theatre." It was just as well not to tread on dangerous ground when the Allies were so near Rome.

Saturday June 3rd

Always those guns. Always nearer. Planes are fighting over the city and the sound of anti-aircraft guns alternates with that of machine guns. The Germans have placed heavy artillery in the southern suburbs and are preparing to make a stand, so it looks as if they might try to hold the city. In that case, as the Allied Command stated today on the radio, "the necessary military measures will be taken to eject them."

Valmontone is taken—at last! The Allies are pouring into the plain that surrounds Rome like water through a dyke. We know from the B.B.C. that in England and in America they are fairly worried about us here in Rome today. Of course anything may happen. We realize that. Yet, apart from the sound of guns, Rome is as quiet as on any other June day, in any year. Quieter, in fact, because there are fewer men in the streets. Women are going about in their summer frocks (carefully "turned" and re-made since last year), groups are drawing water from the emergency fountains, and beggars continue begging and getting their lira from every passer-by. Rome is not looking her best, with her closed shops, dirty pavements and shortage of water, but the weather is exquisite and her churches and monuments are unchanged, while Father Tiber goes on his way through the city as he did two thousand years ago.

Although many Germans left yesterday, at present the hotels near the Station are crowded with them. They must be those who have come in from the Castelli on their way north. All last night heavy vehicles, tanks and lorries rumbled northward through the streets, Via Cassia, Via Salaria, and Via Flaminia being still open for them. Yesterday, near here in Piazza Fiume, Germans systematically emptied a hardware shop, packing all the goods very carefully in a covered truck, so as to travel without shifting and to take the smallest space possible.

There are very few newspapers, and no news in them, but people struggle for them just the same. The confidential instructions to the editors for today's issues ran: "While the battle for Rome is in progress, please emphasize the fact that, whatever may happen, we are not unprepared, and, since the tragic situation which came about last September, we have foreseen all eventualities, even the most painful ones." Having sent out this message, Alfred Cucco, "Minister of Popular Culture," bolted. But not soon enough; for the patriots awaited him, and got him.

And that is all for today. The throbbing of guns in the hills has stopped. One feels the silence, as when the engines of a ship stop suddenly in the night.

Are you imitating the small boy who whistled when going down a dark alley when you want to repeat to yourself and to others that it will be all right? That the Germans will cease upon the midnight without pain, will run northward, will fade out of Rome silently, will fold their tents like the Arabs, or however else the poets would express it? Yes, I think it is a comfort to do so, or even to write it. Here goes, again: *I do not think that the*

Germans will make Rome a battlefield. (But the fighting is very close tonight.)

Sunday June 4th

This has been a day of such stirring experiences that they will perhaps "break through language and escape" before they can be written down. They are joint experiences, put together when we pooled our impressions and information; so much happened in so many directions. We had been suddenly deprived of the telephone (cut off); of newspapers (not out); of the radio (electric current cut off); of trams and buses (for the same reason); but the grapevine information service began functioning with incredible efficiency, and it soon became clear that the famous elastic defence had begun in Rome; the Germans were quietly on the run. When the Romans had grasped the situation, unobtrusively and ironically they began to stroll about the streets mainly used for German traffic. They made no remarks, but looked on with Olympian serenity. This attitude may have been helped by the shower of leaflets from General Alexander which had fallen in the early morning on some parts of the city. They ran as follows:

HEADQUARTERS OF GENERAL ALEXANDER
Special Message to the Citizens of Rome.

The Allied Armies are nearing Rome. The liberation of the city will take place soon. The citizens of Rome must stand shoulder to shoulder to protect the city from destruction and to defeat our common enemies: the Germans and the Fascists.

These directions come to you, Romans, from General Alexander's Headquarters and from Marshal Badoglio. They are given in your interests as well as in those of the Allies.

Do everything in your power to prevent the destruction of the city.

Prevent the explosion of mines which may have been placed under bridges and Government buildings, under the Ministries and other important edifices.

Protect the central telephone and telegraph plants, the broadcasting stations and other lines of communication.

For your own use safeguard the public services: gas houses, aqueducts and electric power stations.

Protect the railways, goods stations and all public transport services such as trams and buses.

Hide your food reserves.

Note carefully the location of enemy mines and war material and inform the Allied patrols of their positions.

Remove barriers and obstructions from the streets.

Leave free passage everywhere for military vehicles.

It is vital for the Allies that the troops should pass through Rome without hindrance or loss of time, in order to complete the destruction of the German army which is retreating northwards.

Citizens of Rome, this is not the time for demonstrations. Obey these directions and go on with your regular work. Rome is yours! Your job is to save the city, ours is to destroy the enemy.

CITIZENS OF ROME. THESE ARE YOUR DIRECTIONS.
THE FUTURE OF THE CITY IS IN YOUR HANDS!

So, with admirable restraint, the Romans looked on, spectators of the reverse of what they had seen in September: the boot was on the other leg, the wheel had gone full circle, and the defeated Huns were escaping in disorder. Along Corso Umberto, Via del Babuino, Via di Ripetta, Corso d'Italia and above all on Via Flaminia crowds stood on the pavements, sat on the steps of churches or in the doorways of palaces or at the tables of the few cafés that were still open. The Germans went on, wild-eyed, unshaven, unkempt, on foot, in stolen cars, in horse-drawn vehicles, even in carts belonging to the street cleaning department. There was no attempt at military formation. Some of them dragged small ambulances with wounded in them. They went, some with revolvers in their hands, some with rifles cocked. On Corso Umberto when one of them stumbled his rifle went off and caused a panic among the crowd; for a moment there was some indiscriminate shooting. Whereas last September they came with machine guns trained on the Romans, it was a different matter now. They were frightened. They had a clear idea of the strength of the underground movement, the power of the armed patriots and their determination to take action when and if necessary. Most of the "Republicans" had fled the day before, but in the German rout were to be seen handsome motor-cars with Fascist dignitaries looking anything but dignified in their anxiety to get away. Some Blackshirt soldiers, members of

[195]

the pitiable Barbarigo and Nettuno Divisions, were desperately waving to occupants of German motor cars, begging for a lift. The latter, true to their custom, as in Russia and in Africa, had no pity on the men whom they had used as tools while despising them, and passed on, unheeding. The crowd showed a good deal of self-control in not lynching these remnants of the Fascist gangs. Two of them, who tried to climb up on a gun carriage in Piazza del Popolo, were kicked off by German parachute men. Near Porta San Paolo, at about midday, there was a panic among the Germans rushing in from the Castelli, when an Allied plane swooped down and attacked them, and they ran wildly toward the Colosseum, seeking cover. The detachments going north along Via Aurelia were watched by Allied reconnaissance planes, and when they were well beyond the city limits, other planes dived at them with machine guns.

At 5.30 this morning, when the regular traffic police reported for duty, they were curtly told to remove the Fascist rods-and-axe badge from their collars and to replace it with the five-pointed star of Italy, "by Badoglio's orders." That was one of the earliest thrills of the day. People whispered to each other "*Hanno rimesso le stellette*," "They've put back the little stars." Even the ultra-Fascist P.A.I. police had changed them, too.

German sentinels with machine guns and tanks guarded all the city bridges until dusk.

At about eleven o'clock in the morning there was such an explosion that the houses near us, including our own, seemed to rise slightly, curtsey and sit down again, a very queer feeling. It was the Germans blowing up the Macao barracks (sometimes called the Castro Pretorio) where they had large stores of petrol and explosives. There were three heavy detonations, and householders in the vicinity trembled lest, at this last moment, they too should be involved in ruin.

A current report ran that the Germans had promised the Pope that they would not destroy anything in Rome if he would be personally responsible for the welfare of the wounded whom they might leave behind; another was to the effect that General Bencivenga, Commander in Chief of the underground forces of the district of Rome, appointed by Badoglio, had given Kesselring to understand that if his men were to blow up the Roman waterworks not one of his wounded would be given so much as a drop of water afterward. Whatever truth there may have been in these rumours, certainly the Germans destroyed all they could in their hasty flight.

Worse than the destruction of the Macao barracks was the blowing up of the Fiat works in Viale Manzoni, which covered a whole city block and which comprised the largest repair shops in Rome for armoured cars and tanks. When this was done several civilian dwellings were wrecked and their owners buried beneath the ruins. The EIAR Roman broadcasting centre in Via Mondello was only partly destroyed, owing to the skill of Filippo Blasucci, a patriot engineer who removed the detonators from mines. In the Campo Verano cemetery, already damaged by Allied bombs, and over which the Germans had held up horrified hands and shed torrents of crocodile tears, they blew up six large plots where they had stored ammunition, causing some casualties among civilians who happened to be there at the time. The Tiburtina, the Prenestina and the San Lorenzo railway yards were destroyed, together with surrounding buildings. The telephone plant was blown up at the Ministero delle Comunicazioni, and in Piazza Regina Margherita they set fire to a lorry loaded with ammunition which exploded and wrecked neighbouring houses. At the railway station in Via Marsala numbers of small buildings were set on fire and railway carriages destroyed.

Only lack of time and the skill and courage of patriots prevented the destruction of many public buildings, bridges and waterworks. Ponte Tazio, a wide modern bridge which spans the Aniene at Via Nomentana and leads to Monte Sacro, would have been completely demolished if patriots had not removed the detonators from five out of the six mines placed beneath it. The reservoir near Santa Croce was completely destroyed. The Roman telephone installation in Palazzo Viminale was saved through quick action on the part of a group of patriot sappers who neutralized 212 pounds of nitroglycerine located in the cellars, sufficient to wreck the whole neighbourhood. On hearing distant explosions, it was difficult to know if they were land mines or big guns. The roads leading to Rome which were bordered with trees had all been mined with an ingenuity worthy of a better cause. At the root of each tree the explosive had been so placed that the trunk would fall directly across the road and constitute a most efficient barrier. The electric wiring which connected the caps of these mines was somewhat complicated; the Germans did not reckon on the speedy retreat forced on them. There was no time to cope with the electric connection, and the roads remained open for the Allies.

At half past twelve someone came in and announced breathlessly: "The British are at Porta Maggiore!" No one believed it. It was much too good to be true. It was like something in a dream. So we waited. Yet the signs we had seen in our own neighbourhood pointed to coming events. All morning the Germans from a "command" of theirs had been giving—yes, actually giving away—tins of food, bags of flour, sausages and blankets. When they had gone small boys swarmed over the house and carried off a few chairs that had remained. At Piazza Siena in the Borghese Gardens Germans had been selling sacks of flour for 1,000 lire, we heard. In Via San Basilio a barricade had been hurriedly constructed of furniture, odd red plush armchairs, tables, stools, and chests of drawers topped by rough planks, in front of a second-rate hotel where Germans had lodged. Perhaps it was the work of retreating Fascists; one could not tell.

The next good news to be spread abroad was that the S.S. torture houses in Via Tasso and Via Romagna and at the political wing of Regina Coeli had been broken open and their occupants set free; while Caruso and Koch, the most cruel Blackshirt bosses (the former being the leader of the raid on St. Paul's), had been arrested and locked up for trial.

By five o'clock in the afternoon the streets were almost empty of Germans; a few were still going along Corso d'Italia, making for Via Flaminia. Everyone knew that the patriot police force, organized and ready for action, had been summoned for 9 o'clock. A strange order was vaguely circulated that the curfew was fixed for 6 o'clock, and all must remain indoors after that time. No one paid the slightest attention to it. One of the few P.A.I. police still to be seen told us that it had been ordered, but his tone lacked conviction. Someone told us an incredible tale that, owing to the Pope's intervention, the Allies would not enter the city until midnight, to give the Germans a chance to retire.

What is much more likely, in fact universally held as true, is that owing to the Pope's efforts the Germans did not make a stand in the streets of Rome and reduce it to the condition of Cassino. At least it was owing to the Pope that such was the decision made by Kesselring, but of course the German flight was hastened when the Allies broke through their defences in the Alban Hills and spread like a torrent in the plain surrounding Rome. So it came about that as the last Germans were fleeing from the city, the Allied patrols were entering, cautiously at first, swiftly and confidently afterward.

Dusk fell, and with it our vicinity grew quiet; but at ten o'clock voices were heard, and footsteps in the street. *"Viva Savoia! viva gli Alleati!"* The men of the underground front were rallying in force. Armed, disciplined and wearing badges with the Italian colours, they were everywhere, ready to round up the straggling Germans and Fascists and to keep order if necessary.

From one of our windows we looked down on Rome. The electric light which had been cut off was turned on abruptly, and uncurtained windows flashed out brightly like a signal of liberation to come. Then, as if on the stage, all was dark once more; except for the moonlight shining through a veil of mist. Suddenly, from the direction of Porta Pia, came a burst of wild cheering. The Allies had entered Rome. The sound of cheering followed the line of Via Venti Settembre as far as Piazza Venezia. After that the whole town came to life. There was talk and laughter in all the streets, even in the narrowest ones; there was cheering and the sound of clapping everywhere.

Later, we heard about what others had seen. How, near the Island in the Tiber, American tanks had stolen in like shadows, their crews peering into the dark, apprehensive of booby traps and German snipers; how they were taken for Germans at first, and how, when at last they were recognized, the welcome they got nearly overcame them.

Fifth Army men arrived in Piazza Risorgimento while German stragglers still occupied the heights of Monte Mario. Some came in along Via Ardeatina and entered at Porta San Paolo; from Via Casilina and Via Prenestina they came through Porta

Maggiore; from the Appian Way by Porta San Giovanni, as the Huns came in September. Finally from Via Appia Antica they entered through Porta San Sebastiano.

In several places there were skirmishes with the belated German rear-guard. Machine guns rattled in Piazza Santa Maria Maggiore and near the Colosseum at about 9 o'clock. The column that came through Porta Pia, and whose welcome we heard, went straight on through the city in pursuit of the enemy, and did not even stop for food or rest. There was fighting on some of the bridges. At about 11 P.M. some Americans fell at Ponte Sublicio, and on Ponte Margherita German dead lay all night.

Wherever the troops entered they were cheered, applauded and showered with blossoms. A rain of roses fell on men, guns, tanks and jeeps. An exuberant Italian rushed forward, took an embarrassed American infantryman in his arms, kissed him on both cheeks and returned home with the bridge of his nose severely cut by the rim of his hero's helmet.

Monday June 5th

The tumult and the shouting died at about 1 A.M., and we scattered from our observation post.

My own first sight of the Allies was dramatic in its simplicity. Opening a window at about 6 o'clock, I saw one little jeep with four American soldiers in it, making its way slowly and soundlessly along the street. No one else was about. The thing looked so solitary, yet so significant in the cool stillness of dawn. I had it all to myself for a few seconds. It was so small, yet so secure; a vignette on a page of history; a full stop at the end of a chapter of oppression and fear.

After breakfast two of us went out on business. Approaching Via Veneto was like stepping from a sullen world of pain, fear, suspicion, concealment and misery into a brave, gay world of high achievement, courage, confidence and chivalry. British and American flags floated in the wind, in the brilliant setting of that wide thoroughfare alive with Allied soldiers. Two long lines of American infantry were marching up either side of the roadway, toward Porta Pinciana. They were dusty, battle-worn and unshaven, but they smiled and waved in response to the greetings of the crowd. They had roses in the muzzles of their rifles, and miniature Italian flags which had been thrown to them; they had roses stuck in the camouflage nets of their helmets, and in their shirts. One has read of these things in books, and accepted them as fiction, never dreaming of witnessing them as we did today. In between the lines of infantry were jeeps, radio cars, ammunition carriers, staff cars and every military vehicle imaginable. They came irregularly, sometimes two or more together, causing a traffic block when they had to turn round. And every car was sprinkled with roses. It looked as if all the pink ramblers in Rome had been requisitioned for the occasion. (Later in the day we gave a big bunch of them to a friend who wanted something to throw to the Allied troops.) Whenever a car passed the crowd on the pavement clapped. When a plane came over, flying low, seemingly out of sheer joie de vivre, they clapped too; and in between they laughed and talked and congratulated each other.

The population of Rome seemed double what it had been; men who had been hiding for months—patriots, Italian soldiers, Allied prisoners of war who had escaped from their prison camps, young men of military age and persecuted Jews—were out and about. Bicycles appeared from their hiding places as if by magic. Rome had not seen such animation and laughter since the beginning of the war. Yet, today in all this joyful effervescence, this relief, this reaction from the horrors of Nazifascism, there was an amazing absence of the rowdy element which so easily predominates on like occasions, as for example on Armistice Day, at the end of the last war.

When we returned we hoisted our own flags on our house, amid the applause of enthusiastic passers-by. People we knew and people we didn't know came in to say they were proud of the Allies and to shake hands and to talk English, and even when they couldn't they talked something they called English, just the same. At the same moment, 10 A.M., Colonel John Pollock hoisted the Union Jack on the Capitol.

Like occurrences were taking place all over Rome on a larger scale. The Scots piped themselves down Via Nazionale to Piazza Venezia, where they gave a concert, amid howls of enthusiasm. Italians who had never seen kilts before admired "the charming little skirts" they wore. The French paraded along Via dell'Impero to shouts of "Vive la France!" British units came up Via Ludovisi in triumph. American soldiers hoisted a big Italian flag on the balcony of Palazzo Venezia, the famous balcony whence the Duce used to harangue the assembled multitudes (summoned by postcards to a "spontaneous demonstration of loyalty"). Down the Corso men of the Fifth Army passed all day to the sound of ceaseless cheering. In reply they tossed American candy to sugar-starved children, and cigarettes to men accustomed to a desperately meagre ration of tobacco.

A camp was established in Villa Borghese, and army cooks got down to the job of preparing meals for the troops. The situation was summed up by our greengrocer's wife (she had had neither greens nor groceries to sell for weeks): "There's nothing to eat, but at least we can breathe!"

Unanimously the thoughts of the Romans went out to the Pope; he had played a large part in saving their city; he had protected them from the terror of battle in their streets; they would thank him. At 7 A.M. and again at 10 o'clock exultant crowds went to Piazza San Pietro calling out for him. Both times he appeared at his study window, acknowledged their greetings and blessed them. A plane circled low at the same moment and dropped flowers.

However, these two visits were not enough. A monster meeting was organized for the evening. As there were still no telephones, no trams nor any of the normal means of communication, in the early afternoon runners spread the news from house to house, and carts and lorries frothing over with boys and bunting and carrying placards: "Come to St. Peter's at six o'clock to thank the Pope" drove through the town in every direction.

By 5 o'clock, from all parts of the town, masses of people were converging on St. Peter's. As they went, they shouted and waved their welcome to Fifth Army tanks and lorries entering the city. Piazza San Pietro was already full when we arrived. The afternoon sun slanted across the roof of the Basilica, spilling torrents of golden light on the sea of colour below. With the flags and banners, it looked like a herbaceous border in full bloom. Soldiers in battle dress provided an olive-drab background for the whole.

A roar of acclamation rose when, after the great bell had pealed and the ceremonial drapery had been flung over the parapet of the central balcony, the slender white-clad figure of the Pope appeared. Presently he raised his hand for silence, and spoke. Every phrase of his was punctuated with thunders of applause, and each time he waited patiently for it to subside before continuing. It was one of the shortest public discourses he ever made, and in its utter simplicity went straight to the hearts of his hearers. He said that, whereas yesterday Rome was still fearful for the fate of her children, today she rejoiced, with renewed faith and hope, in their safety. Therefore, while rendering the most profound homage and grateful thanks to God for this great benefit; while thanking Our Lady for once more showing herself to be in truth the "Salvation of the Roman people," and Saints Peter and Paul for protecting the city once watered by their blood, he begged all to show themselves worthy of the grace received, by ordering their lives in conformity to the standards demanded by the seriousness of the times. Especially would he ask them to put away all feelings of anger and revenge, and to cultivate instead the spirit of brotherly love, of moderation, and of practical compassion for the poor and the suffering. "Lift up your hearts!" he concluded, "and let your answer be: 'We have lifted them up to the Lord!' " He then gave the Apostolic Blessing to the kneeling crowd which continued to acclaim him long after he had left the balcony.

When the gathering broke up it seemed as if the whole Fifth Army had mingled informally with the whole of the Roman population. Leaving the Piazza was a slow business. One had the impression of moving along, up to the waist in jeeps, driven so quietly and with such careful skill among the multitude that they troubled one no more than perambulators. They were friendly little conveyances, and in them were friendly soldiers. Farther on, beyond the limits of the Piazza were military trucks and arms carriers. In the absence of trams, buses and taxis, everyone went home on foot. For many it was a matter of five or six miles there and back, not to mention the standing in the Piazza. But apparently no one minded. Quite the contrary. They didn't mind anything. Fascism was gone; Nazism was gone; and the horror of war had passed from Rome.

[203]

Italy is on the eve of a new era. She has suffered in the crucible of pain and humiliation. She will put her affairs in order and begin life afresh. May her future leaders remember the words of David, spoken long ago:

"Unless the Lord build the house, they labour in vain who build it."